TO GOD
THE GLORY

TO GOD THE GLORY

by

Annalee Skarin

DeVorss & Company
P.O. Box 550
Marina del Rey, California 90294

TENTH PRINTING, 1984

ISBN: 0-87516-094-8

Printed in the United States of America by
DeVorss & Company
P.O. Box 550
Marina del Rey, California 90294

This book should only be read
after the book "Ye Are Gods".

PREFACE

Behold, I, Jesus Christ, the Alpha and Omega, the Beginning and the End, the Great Amen, have commanded Annalee Skarin to write these, my words, and to send them forth unto the ends of the earth, that, you, who know my voice might be prepared to enter into the New Day—that you might be purified even as I Am pure. For this is my commandment unto you, and I give no commandment save I prepare the way for its fulfillment.

This work is given that all my holy promises might begin to be made manifest in very deed, yea, that they might begin to be fulfilled in you, for the time is at hand, even the great day of preparation, the day of Almighty God. the Father.

CHAPTERS

CHAPTER I.

THE KEY OF THE KINGDOM

LET THIS record be as a symphony of music played upon the heart-strings of men's souls. Let its love reach out into the darkest corners of the earth and heal the anguished cry of deep despair and suffering. Let Light arise in every consciousness. Yea, open your souls to this Light of Christ, which is given to abide in every man who cometh into the world. Let its glory of healing Divine compassion, its unspeakable tenderness, its wholeness of complete restoration and its glory of awakening shine forth in every cell and fibre of your souls.

Yea, my beloved, awaken to the call of the New Day! Let wisdom reach its measure of unfolding as you hear my voice and seek refuge beneath my outspread wings, responding to that eternal invitation of infinite, penetrating warmth, "Come unto me all ye who labor and are heavy laden and I will give you rest—". Oh beloved, "how often would I have gathered you, even as a hen gathers her chickens under her wings, and ye would not."

TO GOD THE GLORY

My beloved ones of earth, know ye not that no hen goes out gathering up her chickens one by one? Nay. She draws down, near to earth, and spreading out her protecting wings gives forth her tender call and all that are hers hear her voice and come to her. Then nestling down beneath her wings they add their warmth to hers. Thus secure and snuggled close in the arms of her loving comfort the dark night passes, the storm is unfelt, the danger disarmed, the cold unknown. Such is my call to you, oh earth-born sons! And such is my love! This invitation is not just once for a lifetime. It is for every moment of danger, of sorrow, dismay or distress. I am ever waiting with my outspread wings of eternal love.

For you who come there is no rebuke, no censure, for in my love thy wounds are healed, thy way made straight, thy efforts glorified. For "I am the way, the Truth and the Light!" I am the voice of conscience in thy own being. I am the sacred hopes that burn within thy heart. I am the divine longings in thy soul. I am the righteous desires in thy thoughts, the love within thy heart, the joy that sings in ever-lasting glory and which you hear vibrating upon the very fibres of your innermost beings whenever you draw near unto me.

Yea, truly, "My kingdom is not of this world." My kingdom is of the soul and the kingdom of the soul is the kingdom, known of old, as heaven. And so, I say, "The kingdom of heaven is the eternal kingdom of the soul. This is the kingdom of "oraneous" or expansion, for always the healing and the growth and the expanding comes from within.

Draw near unto me and I will unfold the hidden mysteries known of old, even the "Mystery of Godliness", or the mystery of becoming God-like. And as you open up your hearts and minds unto my voice all that has harassed you will be dissolved. Yea, healing will enfold your troubled minds, your saddened hearts, your wounded bodies, your broken lives. Yea, come and learn the mystery of love and the power of its restoring touch.

Love must first be shed forth from your own hearts e'er it can return unto you, for my love can only enfold you as it begins to flow through you. You are its fountain, or the vehicle through which it flows, which mayhap has run dry because of your negatives which have blocked up the way to the free out-flowing love divine. This great love is ever seeking an outlet through which to flow in its rich, pure, singing abundance. This glorifying love must needs pour forth through the unsealed, open hearts of men. It is truly the broken or open heart that is its vehicle of outlet. Yea it is through an unsealed, open heart that my great love must go out to heal and bless a world.

Know, beloved ones, that hardened, sealed hearts are barren and unproductive in my vineyard. They are fountains run dry. They are cisterns cracked and broken, filled with refuse and debris.

Oh, blessed ones, know that the first of the seven seals, the seals upon the book, which none could remove save me, are the seals within yourselves. The first seal is the one upon your hearts. It has been placed there by the traditions of the fathers, by your own stubbornness, by your lack of tender, melting love. This seal must be broken, or opened. Yea, it must be melted and removed. And it is only by the power and Light of my help within that it can be removed and the stone rolled away.

The hardness in your hearts is most easily dissolved by love, this Christ-like love made manifest from within.

This is the key: "Love God with all your hearts! And as you love with your hearts know that it does not mean just the heart-organ in your physical bodies, but the whole heart center

of your entire beings. Yea, your hearts means
the very heart center of your souls. It is that
living heart center that is like the center or
heart of a tree. It is the source of life outflowing. Know always that this source of living life
flows forth ever from within. Thus all healing
comes first from within. The wound, the bruise,
the cut, the injury must heal from within first
if the healing is to be perfect and endure. And
so must every healing come. Your ills, your
hates, your evils and despairs must first find
that source of living light within and only by
this method can the great healing come. Know
that in your very heart centers is contained that
Light of Christ which was given to abide in
every man who cometh into the world. Open
up your hearts and let it pour forth in love to
heal and bless and glorify.

As you open up your hearts, through love,
you shall begin to know the glory of my words
and the power thereof. Yea, fulfill and live the
law of love and you shall comprehend the very
powers of eternity, even the Light of Christ
which is given to abide in you, and which is
governed by my love.

Love God with all that innermost power of
completeness and you shall have touched upon
the very fibres of your own souls and contacted

[15]

the centers of your own inner beings. Thus, through this Light of Christ, given to abide in you, the seals can be removed to prepare the way of Light, even the Light of Christ, that it might come forth. This is your key.

So it is that the fountain in your own souls can be opened wide to the great outpouring love of God. And as it is shed forth in your own hearts it must first go through every cell and fibre of your own beings bringing its healing and its joy and its great power of eternal renewal. Its singing ecstasy can only be understood by those who are treading the King's Highway. I Am the Way, and my Highway is the Highway of heaven. It is the way to the kingdom within, the kingdom of the soul, or the Spirit, for it is a Spiritual Kingdom, and is not of the flesh.

As you take my words into your hearts and strive to fulfill them love increases and pours out through every cell and fibre of your beings and you will become filled with the unspeakable glory of its redeeming Light and begin to comprehend all things.

As the seal upon the heart is broken and that divine center is softened and opened, or unsealed, the outpouring love of God begins to enter the mind and will remove its seal of blindness.

Glory and praise be unto the Father forever and forever, for His path is made straight and His way of Truth and Light revealed, for as the mind is opened another seal is loosed and that great blindness of mind which has nearly destroyed a world will begin to be removed from you, and you will be given faith and vision to behold the things of God and understand His holy promises. As this Holy Light begins to penetrate the mind His divine vision of perfection is revealed. And with that vision comes the testimony of the Holy Spirit of Promise bearing witness to your souls that it can be fulfilled unto you for you will receive strength to follow it through to its completion. This is the road I mapped, for I Am the Way, even the road of perfection, the path you must follow.

Oh, man of earth, do you not know that it is you who receives the reward and the glory of loving me with all your hearts? Do you not see that as your hearts are opened wide to pour out love to me it is like a syphon that draws upon the great store of eternal love and sets it in motion to help restore yourselves, your broken lives, and flowing out from you go forth to help heal a world? For so it is that the great outpouring glory of God's love flows through your hearts, your souls, your minds, and sweeping the earth it flows on back to God, who is its source. As it returns it is increased and glorified. Back to its beginning it flows in its eternal circle of life-giving fulfillment, increased and intensified to be poured out again upon a world to fructify, to cleanse, to give life and to redeem. This love is pure and undefiled and will give life to you, my children. It will redeem and cleanse the barren, arid spots within your own beings. It will first redeem your own souls, and then go on out to bless all those with whom you associate. Then swinging on out it will help redeem a world and continue on its everlasting pattern, enfold the universe and thus return to the very throne of God. Then with you as an open channel it flows back to you increased a thousand fold and carrying with it all the blessings and powers of God the Father, for within it is the fulfillment of every promise and every desire and all perfection and glory.

Chapter II.

MYSTERY

Oh weary man, submerged beneath your burdens of restrictions, forbidden roads, creeds and orthodoxed "taboos", my hand is yours, my outspread wings invite you to ever draw near and find your strength in safety and in peace. And you who still hunger and thirst after righteousness, did I not promise that you should be filled? Did I not promise that you should comprehend all things? Even the mystery of Godliness? And my word cannot be broken, neither can it return unto me void, nor remain unfulfilled for the day of fulfillment is at hand for those of you who are still hungering and thirsting after righteousness. For you who have continued to ask, to seek and to knock, the doors of righteousness are opening wide. And to you I now reveal these deep and hidden mysteries, these eternal truths that have been hidden since the foundations of the world because of the great wickedness of hardened hearts and blindness of minds.

If you have gone to the banquets of Ephriam

and found the tables filled with naught but vomit, then understand that vomit is nothing but undigested food which has not been assimilated by the body, nor made a part of it. Then, know also that those who have presided over the banquet of the Lord speak forth scriptures which they themselves have not fulfilled nor made a part of their own beings. Such unfulfilled words spoken forth are but spiritual vomit, which defiles the banquet of the Lord. To you who have gone to these banquets and have left them empty and still hungering after righteousness, which is the power of the Lord, I now speak. To you it is given to receive knowledge, and to you it is given to understand doctrine.

These leaders are drunken with the wine and strong drink of power and they err in vision and stumble in judgment.

When I revealed to them the way of rest and the way of refreshing they would not hear.

But you who are weaned from the milk and drawn from the breasts, who hunger and thirst after righteousness, I now speak. Yea, you who have been forced to lie in the bed you have outgrown, the bed in which you can no longer stretch yourselves, and have tried, in vain, to cover yourselves with a covering that has become too narrow, my words ring forth as I ask of you to study prayerfully and very humbly my words given by my servant Isaiah, and recorded in the twenty-eighth chapter of his sacred record. And know that if you have been lulled to sleep in the bed that is too short it is because you have trusted in the arm of flesh, which is not my arm. My arm is the arm of power. And the day is at hand.

Yea, you awakened ones, you still hunger and thirst after righteousness, weep with sorrow for the leaders who are ill with the drunkenness of their own pride and who are "out of the WAY" of the Lord, and who give forth naught but vomit. Yea, weep for the prophet who does not prophesy, the seer who does not see and the revelator who has no power to reveal the mind and will of God but have made lies their refuge. Yea, weep for the drunkards of Ephriam and in loving humility send out thy prayers in their behalf and petition God to hide the shame of their nakedness. Yea, pray for them and condemn them not lest their condemnation fall also upon you. Yea, rather let your hearts be awakened in loving compassion as you plead before the throne of God in their behalf as love pours out through you to bring their healing, if mayhap they will receive it.

Yea, let no anger nor wrath be found in you lest the errors of this generation fall upon your shoulders. And see that ye condemn not.

Yea, my beloved ones, children of the New Day, step forth with me into the great Light, where there is naught but love and compassion and forgiveness, for of you it is now required to forgive all men. Lift up your eyes unto the light and view realms where mortal laws are left behind and the higher laws of God are embraced and fulfilled.

For one moment let me digress and say that I stood beside Thomas Jefferson when he swore upon the altar of Almighty God that he would fight forever any tyranny which endeavored to enslave and rule the minds of men. Today Thomas Jefferson and all the noble and great ones, since time began, stand beside me to destroy this tyranny that is seeking to hold back the progress of men, to enslave their minds and forbids men to come direct to me to receive an answer to their prayers. There are those who deny the power of God to give you such holy answers, and who are denying the power of the Holy Ghost to lead you into all truth, thinking they alone have a monopoly upon the eternal Truth of God.

Pray for such as these but see to it that you

do not permit them to enslave your minds with the force of their power nor the exalted height of their positions, for their arm is flesh. Let none take from you the right to ask, to seek and to knock. Let none take from you the right to come direct to me. It is because of methods such as this that the world has been damned and has remained in its awful state of wickedness and darkness even until now.

To you, my beloved, who fear not the edicts nor the commandments of men, I am now calling. You who are my own will hear my voice and will follow. And I will reveal to you a mystery as I place my hand upon your heads and whisper into the inner recesses of your souls and say, "Look!" "Yea, beloved, look and behold the things long lost from the earth!" For truly "Babylon the great is fallen! Is fallen!"

And so my words come ringing down the ages to find an echo in every softened, vibrant heart, "Babylon the great is fallen! Is fallen!"

Yea, "The great beast that is drunken with the blood of Saints," has reached the end of her power. Yea, this great drunkenness and abhorrence is the drunkenness of power. This is the power which has enslaved the souls and minds of men. It is the power that has slaughtered spiritually and mentally those who have refused to relinquish their minds to enslavement. Yea, and great shall be her downfail. And "Upon her forehead was a name written, MYSTERY, BABYLON THE GREAT, THE MOTHER OF HARLOTS AND ABOMINATIONS ON THE EARTH."

Yea, her name is "Mystery" for she has sought to hide the plain and simple truths of God from the minds of men. Know this, my children, that such have sought always to enfold the Tree of Life in mist as they have continued to "babble-on" in their own assumed greatness. And their children have been harlots with their bastard sons, for they have not borne children unto God. Yea they have borne fruits unknown to the great Creator of the Universe because of the drunkenness of their power and the condition of their darkened minds. For these are they who glory in the honors of the world and in their power to enslave the minds of men and hold them subject to themselves. These are they who serve mammon and not God. These are the ones whose empty hands reach out to hold back those who hunger and thirst after righteousness, who seek to KNOW God and the Mysteries of Godliness and who believe in His promises, and the power of the Tree of Life. These are the ones who have held back the progress of the world since time began. Yea and the blood and sins of this generation will be required at their hands, and of all generations past.

And now they are to be left behind, these blind leaders of the blind, unless they come to me with their broken hearts and in contriteness of Spirit begin to receive of me the blessings which I have held in store for them since time began, blessings which so far exceeds anything they have ever conceived of there is no comparison. Yea, pray for them that they might permit my Light to penetrate into their beings and be healed. Pray for them continually, for it is through your forgiving love and your prayers only that my Light might reach through to their consciousness.

Yea, pray for this earth and the inhabitants thereof. And let love pour out from you to help heal and bless and forgive.

Understand, my beloved, that this love of God, which must be shed forth in the hearts of the children of men, is the very Fruit of the Tree of Life. Yea, this love is the very waters of life. And man is the channel, the fountain, the spring through which it flows. Love is its fulness. Love is the healing power of existence and of the universe. It is this divine love which must flow through you, my children, to be potent with life and healing and renewal. Know this, beloved, you are the channel, or fountain, through which this divine love of God must flow as it goes out in its eternal round to glorify, to redeem, to purify and to exalt and give life and power to all that it touches.

And so again, I gather up my words spoken of old and reaffirm them unto you, my opened and beloved ones; for so I spake to John and said, "Write these words for they are true and faithful. I am Alpha and Omega, the beginning and the end. I will give unto him that is athirst of the fountain of the waters of life freely. He that overcometh shall inherit all things; and I will be his God, and he shall be my son.

But the FEARFUL, and UNBELIEVING, and the abominable, and murderers, and whoremongers, and sorcerers and idolaters and all liars, shall have their part in the lake which burneth with fire and brimstone; which is the second death." (Rev. 21:5-6).

Yea, "And to my beloved ones, the Spirit and the bride say, Come. And let him that heareth say, Come. And let him that is athirst come. And whosoever will, let him take of the water of life freely." (Rev. 22:17)

And why cannot the fearful and those who

are unbelievers have part in the great glory that is to come? Because they have not opened up their hardened hearts, nor sought to anoint their eyes with eyesalve that they might see, yea that the blindness of their minds might be healed. Instead of being vehicles and transmitters for my love they have become dried up fountains, broken cisterns that hold no water, empty wells gone dry in the barrenness of their own souls and they stand in their desolate unproductiveness.

Oh, my children, do you not know that if you had sought me with all your hearts and permitted my love to come forth through you I would have healed you? Know you not that if you had but permitted even a little of my light and love to come forth your seals could have been removed by my power, one by one? First the seal upon your hearts so that love could begin to come forth to remove the other seals; yea the great love that would also bless and restore and heal you as well as the world? As your hearts opened to the inflowing, outflowing power of my love the seal from your hearts would have been completely removed and your hearts would have become open vehicles or transmitters of the love of Almighty God. Next the seal upon your blinded minds would have been dissolved and you would have been given vision of these more perfect laws and would have understood my words. And as your eyes were opened by the removing of your own blindness you would have been given faith to fulfill. for such is my law.

Yea. know ye not that I give no commandment unto the children of men save I prepare the way for its fulfillment? Even the command to be perfect even as your Father in heaven is perfect is not a vain and meaningless command. Yea. "Nothing is impossible to him who believes."

As those first two seals are removed, the hardness from the heart and the blindness from the mind the other five will follow. To all mankind the first two are the same, only for some they are more solid, and more difficult to remove.

The other five seals that remain will automatically follow the releasing of the first two. For each of these other five seals vary according to the weaknesses within each of you. These other seals are your prides and prejudices, your jealousies and fears, your greeds and secret abominations, your lusts and hates and evils. These are seals to your progress and each will be dissolved by the sanctifying glory of my inflowing, outpouring love and light as you permit it to be shed forth through your hearts.

Yea, for you, beloved ones, who have opened up your great heart centers to my love, the doors of my kingdom will be opened. As you love God with all your hearts the great heart center of your souls will open to the glory of the great Christ Light that is continually knocking at the door of your consciousness. And thus is your consciousness awakened and the seal removed from your minds. As this Light of Love is permitted to come forth in you it sweeps all negative forces before it and you will feel yourselves being gradually filled with its divine rays and purified from all your weaknesses, which have been your seals. Within this love and Light of Christ is the glory and the power to fulfill all the promises and to fulfill all things. It is yours to use if you will not doubt nor be of little faith.

For you, my beloved ones, the "mist" enfolding the Tree of Life will be dissolved. For you there need be no more "Mystery" or "Mist-tree" for the Tree of Life will ever be clearly seen and forever and forever shall you have access to the Fruit thereof. For the Fruit of the Tree of Life is the love of God that must be shed forth through the hearts of the children of men. You are the bearers of this Fruit, my beloved. For you Cherubim's flaming sword need never fall. This flaming sword falls only on those who remain in their sins. And when His sword falls, it is death.

However, for you who have followed that Still Small Voice to its source, or who have sought to live the laws and to know of their truth there is no flaming sword, no "Mist-tree". For you the Tree of Life will no longer be surrounded in "mist" and you shall partake of its fruit, which fruit is my love which is shed forth in the hearts of the children of men, when the hardness has been overcome by fulfilling that First and Great Commandment, which commandment was given for your glory and redemption.

Chapter III.

REND THE VEIL OF DARKNESS

Know this, ye sons of Light, that through you also, must the darkness of the earth be overcome. And this great darkness must first be overcome right within yourselves. As you banish the darkness in your own minds and thoughts and hearts so that no vibrations go out in negative form, nor in opposition to the rays of Holy Light, you enter into the greatest work possible to participate in, in this sphere of action. This is the greater works, of which I spake unto mine Apostles of old.

This banishing darkness from one's being means also to overcome all light-mindness, which is but the pastime of those without thought. It means, also, my children, to triumph over fears and all negatives. When the darkness is overcome then faith is perfected and matured and becomes knowledge. And "Knowledge is power."

Know this surely, "Despair cometh because of *iniquity*. "Iniquity" means a lack of inner quiet, or as your original language would have expressed it, "lack of inner quiety". It is a lack of that contact with the divine power of God within. It is the outward racing of one's thoughts hither and yon in great disquietude. It is a lack of the great peace acquired by the practice of being STILL and KNOWING God.

Learn to be STILL, and entering into the kingdom of your soul gain your strength and sustenance from me. I Am their author and their source within you. Yea, I, Jesus Christ, Son of the Living God, who was crucified upon the cross, and the source of this Light of Christ which is given to abide in you. From my realm is it shed forth under my jurisdiction, even according to the Will of God, the Father. "Yea, "do all that thou doest in the Name of the Lord, and call upon the Name of the Son forevermore," that you may be blessed in all your doings and that I may increase this divine Light within you, even according to your power to receive.

When dark and evil forces seek to engulf, to confuse, to overwhelm, distress or destroy you, draw near to me and call upon the Father in My Name and thus find your peace and security 'neath my outstretched wings, which "wings" are but symbolical of my outstretched power. Then giving thanks that I have heard and resting in the security of my love let gratitude sing that song of vibrant ecstasy within your souls. And behold! The darkness is gone! And the Son of Righteousness arises with healing in His wings!

These journeys into the realms of dark and Light, are quite necessary, my children. They are necessary so that each of you might find your place and of your own strength learn to hold that place. Yea, that you might overcome the darkness and become bearers of eternal Light.

When you first remove the seal of blindness and the gift of vision is given and you comprehend this greater work, then angels are sent, by my hand, to attend you. Sometimes there are hosts or legions of them attending you. You may not see them, but you will feel their presence and the strength of their sustaining hands. You will feel the music of their glorifying song of divine power, the encouragement of their unheard voices, the love of their hearts. And as they attend you that divine song of ecstasy begins to vibrate in a singing echo of triumphant joy and light within your own hearts. This singing song of ecstasy, of gratitude and thankfulness is my Light swinging into power within you. "The darkness comprehendeth not this Light" and flees from it. And "they who reject this light are under condemnation." And their condemnation is "That they are walking in darkness at noonday," and hear not my voice, nor know me, and are left unto themselves.

As you, beloved, develop that light from within and learn to stand alone in your own strength, the angels, directed from my throne to attend you, are withdrawn and you are left to stand in your own strength that you may become strong and sure and that you might learn to discern between the darkness and the Light. It is also that you might learn of the power of God, and the power of mammon, or earth. Again and again, mayhap, these blessed ones are sent to lift you up and give you support and strength. For from the time you receive the vision of this divine work there are special ones assigned to assist you until you become one with the Light and find your own place and learn to walk therein, in your own strength. Yea, how else could you become strong in the Light and be Master of It unless you learned to overcome the darkness?

Each of you, my children, must learn to stand alone. Each of you must learn to walk alone. You must learn to pick yourselves up and step forth in your own strength and walk out into these glorified realms of eternal Light.

As an earthborn child finds its strength and steps forth, at first in trembling anxiety, know that so must you learn to stand upright and walk. And as you progress the whole universe looks on and rejoices in your final achievement as you step out beyond the mortal stage of infant progress and childish human laws.

As you stand upright you view with higher vision and new worlds await the treading of your feet. It is even as when an infant takes its first baby steps, which experience has been repeated as many times upon this earth as a child has learned to walk. The family, standing back, gives encouragement and breathless solicitude to the wee one beginning the great adventure of a new life with its faltering, halting steps. It takes but a few steps alone to give the little one confidence and reveal to it the power contained in its toddling feet as it masters the science of standing upright and walking forth into new realms and conditions. The whole family rejoices in the thrill of the baby's achievement as another member of humanity steps forth from infancy into childhood.

Your stepping forth into the Light, my beloved ones, is far greater than the infant rising from its crawling position to stand and walk erect. Yea, all the heavens rejoice in your achievement as new and greater scopes become your heritage in your eternal progress and advancement.

It is at this point twixt the rising and the falling, or the darkness and the Light that the mortal attitudes and mind of groveling, crawling, earth-bound man are left behind. Thus standing upright in the majesty of your own soul you can step forth in your march toward glorified divinity, the "Life more abundant." This is the life I promised and this promise must be fulfilled unto you who live by the higher laws of a higher kingdom, which is not of this world. To you is the victory of fulfilment if you will but follow me for my arms are open wide to receive you in my eternal love.

So you see, my beloved, as you overcome the darkness in your own selves and cast out the fears and jealousies you can begin to be endowed with divine power, for as you overcome the darkness within yourselves you will receive power to help rend the veil of darkness that covers the earth. This is the task for which your strength was developed and for which it was destined. Yea, this is the work at hand.

Come ye, my children of the New Day, and lifting up your hearts, banish the darkness. Yea, banish it by love and praise and deep gratitude and as this song of ecstasy arises in your hearts you will know that I am there. Know that it is this singing song of gratitude and great out-pouring love and joy that contacts my powers and brings them into immediate action right within you.

Yea, for you, my beloved children of Light, there are no mysteries. The "mist-trees" are for those who cling to old ways and old paths and walk in the traditions of their fathers. The "mist" is for those who have no desire nor will to ask, to seek, or to knock, nor any faith in me nor in my promises, nor in my great power of fulfilment.

But for you seeking ones, the "mist" is dis-solved and the great mystery is revealed as the great Tree of Life. Yea, the great mist of dark-ness that has covered my earth for ages will be dispelled in you. For when I come you will see as you are seen, clothed in darkness, or clothed in Light. And as you are clothed so will you appear, and so will all things appear unto you. To you who have not overcome the darkness the great Light of my coming will be but dark-ness unto you if that remains your choice and you love the darkness rather than the Light. Yea, if you are thus clothed in darkness you will be blinded by the approaching Light and will fight it with your feeble strength and your blinded bigotry until you yourselves fall in complete exhaustion and utter impotency. For none can fight my Light any more than by their feeble hands they can hold back the rays blazing from the noonday sun.

You, dearly beloved ones, who are beginning to array yourselves in Light, you will see also as you are seen, and the Light will be the beholding powers of your own exalted vision. So shall you see, just as you are seen, by my holy ones who are even now sent to gather out the tares from the wheat that they might be removed from the earth. The tares are they who have no part with me, who have rejected the Light of Christ, which was given to abide in them, and who see no glory in the great approaching light. These are they who are walking in darkness at noonday.

Chapter IV.

THE ONLY ACCEPTABLE SACRIFICE

The only sacrifice acceptable to God, from the days of my ministry to this present day has been, as I informed you, the sacrifice of a broken heart and a contrite spirit. From that day on an offering of blood has been an abomination, though appointed anciently in symbology of my sacrifice upon the cross. In its appointed time the symbol was fulfilled, the sacrifice for which the symbol was appointed, for I came and fulfilled the ancient law. Thereafter such sacrifices were forever ended and were no longer acceptable before the throne of God.

Neither has a sacrifice of one's time, services, his wealth and offerings been able to take the place of the appointed sacrifice henceforth required at the hand of man. Know this, beloved, the only complete, acceptable sacrifice is the appointed one which our Father hath ordained, even the sacrifice, or offering, of a contrite Spirit and a broken, or open heart.

This sacrificial offering alone involves the complete surrender of the "self" to me. It demands the sacrifice of your pride, your personal opinions, your bigotry, your errors and mistakes. Yea, this is the only acceptable offering, the only sacrifice worthy of the fulfilled promise of My Life sacrificed upon the cross for you, even the Lamb slain from the foundation of the world. This sacrifice of my life was the pattern by which your own lives could be perfected. My life surrender but portrays the offering of the little, mortal self, the complete surrender of your misguided wills to the great and Holy Will of your Father. This sacrifice that is required of you crucifies your selfish traits, your sensual lusts and fulfills the utter surrender of even your pain and anguish and suffering and heartbreaks to me.

Those who think they can serve me fully in any other way than by this appointed offering of a broken, or breaking heart, and in a spirit of humbled and subdued devotion are laboring in vain. This sacrifice is the complete surrender of your wills to the will of God.

No high positions, that feed your pride, no endless years of service, no tithes nor offerings, no filling of missions can fulfill the great law, nor provide the necessary sacrifice of acceptability. These services and offerings are but minor contributions, though you give all your time and your talents, though often they will help you to find the way to offer up your broken hearts to me, they are not the fulfilling of the law. Of themselves they hold no power upon my altar for these services are not the appointed offering ordained at the hand of my Father. And until you have given the "self" or your personal "will" in complete and utter surrender, in contriteness of spirit, and your broken or opened hearts, your works have no power or efficacy and your sacrifices are mostly vain as far as the fulfilling of the law is concerned.

Only the complete surrender of the "self" or your own "will" through the open heart and with a humble spirit can fulfill the required law of sacrifice and prepare you for your anointing of the Divine Light of Christ.

The release of your broken hearts contains all the outpouring burdens of your past mistakes, your pride and weaknesses and failures, and the complete and utter surrender of your immature, erring wills.

When you, beloved, have learned the power of this required sacrifice and abide by this sacred law your mortal selves will step aside and you will be prepared to receive the divine anointing of Light and the joy of my fullness. You will no longer be afflicted with the deadly "I" diseases that have blinded my children for ages, for you will be healed. Yea, my dearly beloved, you will become open channels through which my love can pour forth to help bless and heal a world.

Know this, my chosen and elect, the easiest, simplest way to get the right attitude in which to offer up your broken hearts is through a daily, hourly practice of that First and Great Commandment, for in it are all the keys of righteousness and the divine keys of fulfilment. The heart is softened through love and prayer and its seal is broken and it is opened wide to the full outpouring of my divine love.

Then expanding that great love to the soul, that you might love with all the soul, brings a contriteness of Spirit that is overwhelming. It brings with it the baptism of tenderness, compassion, forgiveness and holiness. It is a surrender of soul that is bathed in tears, not tears filled with anguish and despair, nor tears fraught in desperate agony, but the fruitful, life-giving, joyous tears of renewal and singing ecstasy as all anguish and sorrow and despair is released unto the Lord. This is the surrender of your broken heart, that the love and Light and glory of God's great love might take its place.

Then this great love that is shed forth through your heart, diffusing your soul, penetrates and fills your mind the blindness thereof will be removed and you will begin to comprehend all things, even those great and mighty things that have been hidden from the foundation of the world. Yea, you will begin to have a part in their fulfilment, for they will be fulfilled in you.

As you learn to stand in the Light you will be filled with Light. Your great burden of "self" will be turned over to me and being held in the flame of love flowing forth from the center of your souls it shall be reborn, a "new creature". Yea, it will be born of love and born of God. For so it is that the purifying flame of love, as it pours through your own open heart and contrite Spirit, will purify your life and cleanse your soul. This inner flame removes the weaknesses, heals the errors, transforms the mistakes. The symbol of baptism is but the symbol of this inner reality.

The old laws are not broken by these greater truths, they are fulfilled in them, for he who fulfills that first great and Holy Commandment, and the second, which is so like unto it they are almost identical, will have fulfilled all the laws and kept all the commandments. For such there is no law, or as my servant John proclaimed, "They are no longer under the law."

CHAPTER V.

LEGIONS TO COMMAND

I HAVE TOLD you, my children, that all that I have is yours, and you have not understood my words, nor comprehended the power contained in them. Draw near to me that I might unveil to you the mystery of my words and show you how to use, in intelligence, the powers I have bestowed upon you.

You, my children, now comprehend that there are forces, or powers, invisible to your mortal eyes, which have been explained quite thoroughly in the great Hand Book of Life. "Ye Are Gods". These forces, or powers, though unseen are as real as anything which can be registered upon the five senses you possess.

Know this: hate, love, wind, lightning, cosmic rays, perfume, music and despair are all realities and their forces are generated and massed together as living entities, subject to command.

Some of these forces named above have been a marvel to thinking beings since time began, yet never have they been understood. Nevertheless the forces which are scarcely recognized are often more powerful than those that have continued to challenge men's thoughts since the day that time began.

It is my Word, and my word to man cannot be broken, that all things were to be subjected unto you, and that you should subdue the earth and all the forces thereof. To comprehend the powers behind the wind, to be able to stop the rain or to bring it forth, or to use the powers which I planted in your own souls you must begin to comprehend first the powers of creation contained within yourselves and bring them into subjection to your wills.

These forces which are released from within you, my children, in your ignorance and wrath, or in love and tenderness of soul are living entities, endowed with powers unspeakable. The entities of love, kindliness, compassion and forgiveness lend themselves naturally to obey the laws of the universe and the will of God, in bringing to you automatically your "good". The evil forces you have released have often become your masters and you who created them have been but their defiled breeding ground as they have triumphed over you in torturous tyranny. Yea, in the forces which you have created have been carried your weals and your woes. If your woes have predominated it is because you have not been aware of the caliber nor of the powers you have released by your own rebellious, angry, hate filled thoughts, your secret lusts, your jealousies and fears.

These great forces which have ruled your lives have been released from your own beings and are composed of living entities conceived by your own thoughts as they have mingled with your emotions. Where these two meet, thought and emotion, vibrating together, the very powers of creation are released. And those vibrations which are thus released are actually living entities endowed with power and intelligence. And to these entities of your own creation belong the powers of fulfilment. They are sired by the energy of your own thoughts and conceived in the quivering embrace of your emotions, their mother.

"Emotion" is "Energy-in-Motion". Energy is never static. It is always expressed in motion.

The thought and emotion are two creative forces, the male and female principle, which, when set in motion within you become united and are the parents of the forces which are so dynamic and powerful they have been the redeemers and the enslavers of the human race. When the thinking powers of nations and peoples have degenerated into lusts and greeds and evil desires those nations and people have decreed their own downfall and have themselves fulfilled it.

These forces, or entities, which are thus conceived and born from the womb of man, the "wo-man", are brought forth according to the thoughts which sired them and the emotions which conceived them in her womb and brought them forth as living entities.

Bad thoughts can never set in motion good actions or re-actions, nor can they produce entities of health, prosperity and eternal powers of progress, happiness and well-being.

Neither can good thoughts and emotions produce evil results. Grapes do not grow on thistles, nor figs on thorns.

Each seed or thought produces after its own kind. And the power of its bringing forth is the energy of feelings set in motion at its conception. It may be that they are but weak and incipid entities you are creating and they will but return to weigh you down with a continual tiredness as they ride upon your shoulders. Such incipid, whining entities turn their creators into neurotic, self-pitying individuals.

If behind such sired legions there is great force, they will hold within their hands the fury of their birth, if they are evil, they will return in deadlier ways and with the powers of your destruction in their grasp. These entities come forth with the intensity and power by which they were created and you are their sire, and you are their mother. And they are yours. Know, that within you is the power of production and the power to fulfill the fertility of the seed as your own emotions mother the sperm your thoughts bring forth.

With this knowledge comes a responsibility such as you have never before known. Yea, from henceforth you will be held completely accountable for your every thought, not just your idle thoughts, which have always had the power to judge you, for it is your own thoughts which have condemned you to mediocrity or lifted you to the unbarred ways of infinite success and boundless achievement.

Yea, in this new dawning greater responsibilities will be henceforth placed upon your shoulders, for your graduation from the old earth ways is now at hand. The new, advanced school is opened for your learning as new realms open up their majestic opportunities. In these higher realms every endeavor brings forth its full results.

You, my children, who are permitted to have a part in this New Age of Dawning Light and

Power, ruled by wisdom and love must needs begin to comprehend all things. Yea, for all things must become subjected unto you, both in heaven and on earth, the Light and the Life, the Spirit and the Power, sent forth by the Father, through the great Light of Christ which is given to abide in you. Each of you must begin to exert full control over your own great powers. You must exert the will and the power to bring all things under your feet and have all things begin to obey you, both in heaven and on earth. This is your destiny, and for this were you created.

So it is, my children that the entities which you bring forth and release are the very forces of creation. They are powers and their existence is most real. They go forth endowed with the strength and power under which you produce them. And as they go forth so will they return unto you again. And with their returning they come back multiplied an hundredfold; yea, more.

If your creations have been entities of fear or hate or strident, discordant negatives, which you have released, they will return to find lodgement within your own beings and bring naught but distress and confusion into your surroundings. Their power is disease, which is dis-ease, of body, mind and conditions. Their destructive powers are immeasurable.

Every man is judged automatically and continually by his idle thoughts. Idle thoughts are the wasted seeds of life. They are the very cast-off energy of vibrating Life Itself. If these thoughts are sent out with enough power to mingle with emotions they are no longer idle, but active, and they go forth to produce many-fold the condition under which they were conceived. These vibrations, or entities, or legions, are the living forces of production and existence.

Old age, illness, death and even eventual Spiritual destruction are caused by these forces which man himself creates. Floods and epidemics and disasters are always caused from the forces of man's own creating.

To you, my beloved anointed ones, who, through faith and love can release my light and my love and the powers of perfection within your souls the seals on your hearts and minds will be removed so that the hardness and blindness might be forever overcome and you will step forth in the power of your divine creatorship, producing naught but glory and peace and joy and happiness and thus you will glorify your Father, which is in heaven.

Yea, if you will learn to love God with all

your hearts you will automatically have the hardness melted and the great outflowing of healing Divine love will pour through you to heal and bless and purify yourselves, your conditions—and a world.

This love will go out through your own beings, through your heart centers, then through every cell of your bodies and bring its great power of renewal and purification so that you might truly become my sanctified. Yea, in this great love, this stream of the Waters of Life, you will become cleansed and the blindness of your minds will be removed so that you might begin to comprehend all things. It will be then that you will have the power to understand fully the great vision and promise of perfection, which is so necessary for you to comprehend and desire before you can possibly reach it. As you begin to comprehend that no promise, nor commandment was ever wasted, and that all must be fulfilled and that these things belong to you, if you will only believe them, then will your calling and election be made sure and your goal become a reality. Then you will be prepared to know me.

As the hardness of your hearts is overcome, and the blindness of your minds so that you begin to see the truth and the reality of perfection, then gradually all the other seals will be removed.

There are five other seals, besides those first two, which every individual carries. They are the seals that have held back your progress. They have held mankind so bound to his earthy conditions and influences that he has never been able to fulfill his heritage. Mankind has even been quite satisfied with the groveling condition of misery, despair, illness, continual heartbreaks and eventual death, as its goal, that it has been completely blind to the promises of the Almighty.

The first two seals are the same for all. They are the hardness of hearts and the blindness of minds. These other five seals are varied according to each of you, my children. These last five seals are according to your own inheritance and often your own choosing. They are pride or prejudices, greed, selfishness, hate, discords, malice, jealousy, lust, sensuality or any of the other negative traits concealed within the flesh. Laziness is a seal, so is an inferiority complex, or its opposite, the over-sized ego. You will not have all these faults, but five of them, or others just as binding, are yours in either a lesser or greater degree. Yea, these are the seven seals spoken of in Revelations, which only I could remove. They can only be removed by bringing forth My Light within you, through opening yourselves to my divine love. As this compassionate, forgiving, Christ-like love, carried on the wings of light, flow through you these seals can and will be melted and consumed, one by one. And know this, beloved, when the hardness of your heart is removed the blindness of your mind must follow. And if you will but believe, and continue in your desire to attain unto me the others will be removed, for you will be purified and cleansed by this flame of glowing light flowing through your beings.

Yea, as love is brought forth its burning flame of my Light consumes the seals and purifies the weaknesses and cleanses the entire being of man. In the "contrite" spirit the flame of purification is intensified and by its humility the little mortal self is submerged and forgotten. And thus one can be gradually transmuted into the great reality of love. Yea, "Pray with all the energy of heart that ye might be possessed of this great love—". Yea, pray that you might actually become this love.

If your every thought is of peace and love and mercy and compassion and blessing, these great powers will become the powers of your creating ability. Know fully that the entities which you create multiply the power under which they are conceived. The power under which they are created and born is their heritage and they have the power to enlarge and increase that heritage a hundred fold.

Job learned the power of his thoughts when he confessed, "The thing I greatly feared has come upon me." The things anyone greatly fears will come upon him, for he is their creator and they must return to him again.

Fears, unless overcome by stronger thoughts of confidence and faith, are always fulfilled. But perfect love casteth out all fear. If these vibrations, or original thoughts are of lack, then lack follows. Know you not the meaning of the words, "Trust in the Lord with all thine heart?"

Beloved, if your thoughts and feelings mingle in contrary vibrations to the great celestial symphony of the universe, the symphony of love and peace and good and praise and glory, then are you out of tune with the infinite powers of God. If negatives and ugliness crown your thoughts then you will be producing with your hates and discords and selfishness naught but ugliness, illness, confusion, decay and death.

So it is, my beautiful children, that one becomes an "ogre" or a friendless, discordant being without realizing that he or she created the

[55]

repulsive, adverse conditions which bring about such repellent unwholesomeness, even his own miseries and his woes and his unhappiness, failures and distress.

Love too, is born of these same powers of creation, but it, being in tune with the great power and love of the Father is endowed with infinite healing and unspeakable glory. These entities or forces are the powers of Living Light, clothed in the singing glory of the Infinite. Love returns bringing its gifts and graces. Peace returns with its blessings of abundance, health, happiness and security. Joy brings the very fulness of God. And "Joy is of the Saints."

And so, my beloved sons and daughters, you can swing far out, and, taking hold of the powers of eternity, leave the little earth-bound ways of men and with the powers of creation in your souls begin your work in the higher realms of glory and infinite, complete achievement.

The following quotation is a symphony of holy promise to those who will live by it. These words are my own, and they cannot return unto me void. And remember this also, that with each promise and command there is the power of fulfillment to those who will only believe and take hold of the promises. Yea, take hold of this promise and remember it always: "He who

is thankful in all things shall be made glorious;
and the things of this earth shall be added unto him, an hundred-fold; yea, more."

To "be made glorious?" Ah, words of promise that hold the keys of all perfection hidden
deep behind their outward forms! Yea, beloved,
come and stand beside me and we will pull
aside the veil that you might glimpse the daz-
zling glory with which these words are endowed.
Look! And behold a being clothed in Light! Yea,
see thyself thus clothed in glory and filled with
power! Then look further and see a new race
of men rising out of this day's ashes and con-
flict to fill their places, arrayed in flaming
light! And look beyond and see a whole world
redeemed by such as thee, and these noble ones
of beauty and glory!

Yea, beloved, know that this is in your hands
to fulfill and the Light becomes the Life of
those who overcome the darkness. Remember,
the darkness is the hates, the fears, the discords
and all negative thoughts and feelings right
within your own beings. And as you cast them
out you will be filled with light and comprehend
all things. Yea, all things will become subjected
unto you. You shall become one with the very
power of the Almighty and have access to the

very archives of eternity. This is the power which belongs to him who overcomes.

Never again permit yourselves to be the breeding ground of darkness, evils, discords and distress.

Perfect love casts out all fear, or converts, or transforms the evils thereof into eternal power of infinite magnitude. Yea, perfect love is the divine, transforming power of our Father and holds all things in its tender embrace. One who perfects this gift of love overcomes all negative, evil forces, first within himself, then in his surroundings and then, sending it out it goes on multiplying blessings forever.

Yea, all things will be subjected unto him, both in heaven and on earth, the life and the light, the spirit and the power, sent forth by the Will of the Father through me, Jesus Christ, His Son. And no word can return unto Him void.

The time is at hand for all things to begin to be fulfilled—in YOU!

Chapter VI.

"MY KINGDOM IS NOT OF THIS WORLD"

In my earthly ministry I gave the information that my kingdom was not of this world. Neither are the greater laws, which I imparted, of this earth. Most of the laws, those great unloved, untried laws which I gave are the higher laws of My Kingdom, and are truly not of this world. These higher laws are of an advanced realm and await those who have the vision and courage to accept them and the desire to fulfill them.

It is true, as this world has proclaimed, that the Sermon on the Mount, which I gave, and the First and Second Great Commandments are not meant for mere, dull mortal living. For when they are lived one is no longer either dull nor mere mortal. Remember, my beloved, I promised the world that he who would live the laws I gave would KNOW whether they were of God, or whether they were given without authority or power. Few have accepted the challenge to live the sacred laws of my Kingdom, those Holy laws beyond mortal requirements. Those who have, have not only proved the Source of the laws, but having fulfilled laws beyond human standards they have been admitted into "My Kingdom", which is not of this world.

Those who seek only to see and live by the laws which suit their individual lusts and desires, rejecting the higher laws of My Kingdom, must needs abide upon a lower plane. The selection is entirely their own. Go beyond the stated requirements, the scheduled laws of "righteousness' and learn the great mysteries of Godliness. Laws are not difficult. Laws are but the pathway of your own glory. They are all there from the greatest to the least. You make your own selection of the ones you are willing to obey, thus selecting the kingdom you wish to inhabit. Like the rich young man, who obeyed all the laws of the Kingdom of Heaven, except one, and because he desired his worldly wealth, more than he desired my Kingdom, which was not worldly, he remained in the kingdom to which laws he was completely willing to obey. There are laws telestial, laws terrestial and Celestial laws. And within each of these three main divisions ar many grades and states. You who belong to My Kingdom must needs live the higher laws, and they are the laws that are higher in their purified requirements.

Any and every law is easy to obey when you love me and desire to obey me more than you desire your own petty whims and appetites. If your own lusts are your greatest desires then you will obey the call of the flesh and remain enslaved to your senses, your prides your appetites and carnal cravings.

The laws of My Kingdom, which is not of this world, contains the highest laws possible. Yet even these laws are easy to fulfill and live by if you desire to enter My Kingdom, and believe in the promises I have made unto the children of men.

Few on this earth have been able to live even the lesser laws of the Golden Rule. Those who have are the noble of the earth and have built their characters into monuments of everlasting value and power. The Golden Rule is the highest mortal law given. But I have invited you to reach beyond mortality and have given the laws by which this may be accomplished. Reach beyond mortality and fulfill the divine laws and you will become divine.

The Ten Commandments are the main laws to govern mortal, physical living. The Golden Rule is a law beyond these and is one of inner ethics which is written in a man's own soul. If one cannot live by the Ten fundamental Commandments and mocks at, or rejects them, how can he hope to be prepared to abide the laws of my Kingdom? If one cannot live the Golden Rule how can he hope to fulfill those Two, the First and Second Greatest of all Commandments. Those who can obey the petition to give themselves completely to God and their fellowmen in perfect love will thus fulfill all the lesser laws, and as my servant John, declared, will be truly born of God, and will no longer be under the law.

"My Kingdom is not of this world." Neither are the laws pertaining to My Kingdom of this world. Live the laws which govern my Kingdom and you shall have the power to pass into my Kingdom and become members of the Church of the Firstborn, or the Kingdom of the Firstborn. Yea, you shall belong to the "Righteous, whom I have, and will reserve, unto myself." Then becoming members in the Kingdom of Light, and perfected, you will no longer be under any law, for you will have fulfilled all laws and all righteousness.

"Be ye perfect, even as your Father in Heaven is perfect," is a command of the higher Kingdom, which demands that you forgive your enemies, pray for those who despitefully use you and persecute you, and of whatever is required of you, you must give double. "And that which you do unto the least of these, my brethren, ye do it unto me." "The least" are those whom you may consider unworthy of any consideration or help at your hands. Surely such unworthy ones *are* the "least" and most in need of your compassion.

Hard laws you say. Then you are not prepared to live by them and must go your way, the way of your own choosing, the way of the world.

If to you these laws are beautiful and desirable then you may take my hand and come follow me. To you, my dearly beloved, anointed ones, may I say, that no commandment was ever given by me, or by My Father, which did not contain the power of its fulfillment if you will only continue to desire and believe, for these very words are endowed with the Living Life of my being.

"Nothing is impossible to him who believes." Believe in my promises and they are yours. If you "Keep my commandments, then am I bound." Where your strength and understanding ends then mine will begin.

And do not think that if you turn your "other

cheek" to be smitten by some bully, as you cringe in groveling fear, that you are fulfilling my law. That is not my law. My law demands that you stand before every adversity clothed in the peace of my power, the majesty of my strength, the knowledge of my nearness and with every vibration and thought issuing forth from you in complete control. This is the power of divine dignity, the place of supreme command. Cringing, groveling acceptance, fear and retaliating vibrations of hate and resentment hold naught but the weakness of the coward, or the self-pitying, sanctimoniousness of a weakling. And in such condition or attitude you could be beaten into the mud a thousand and one times and yet not have fulfilled my law. My law is power! Ineffable power! My law is that you hold your thoughts and your vibrations in such complete control, reacting only with love, forgiveness and compassion. Then, no matter what men would do to you, the strength of your own released re-actions would rock the earth.

Live the higher laws in their fulness and receive the power to clothe yourselves in their majesty. And remember first and always that self-righteousness destroys instantly the power of the fulfilling. Only in divine humility and perfect love can one tread the highway of the divine, for straight is the gate and narrow is the way, for it does not include the broad ways of many diverse patterns and evils. It is a pathway that must follow in a straight and true line the Light of my law and of my leading. It is truly a narrow way, lighted by the very glory and power of God and is most beautiful. It does not follow into dark roads and forbidden paths of dismay and evil. It is the highway of joy and achievement and infinite, divine power. It is The Way—the way of God. Walk it humbly, my dearly beloved, and as you tread the sacred road of glory you shall be purified and clothed in light. I Am the Way, and you must needs travel it by My Light.

This is the way of joy and of perfection. This is the pathway of divine ecstasy which brings one to the fulness of God, or joy, which has been promised to those who would lift their eyes unto the heights and follow the Way of my laws for these laws only can prepare you for my Kingdom. He who goes up any other way is a thief and a robber and will be cast out.

Beloved children, you who are permitted to have part in this New Age of Dawning Light and power, ruled by my holy laws in love and wisdom, know that the law is given that you might fulfill the law and pass beyond it, that you too might no longer be under the law. To reach this great love that the laws might be fulfilled it is necessary that you begin to exert full control over your own great powers of creation. You must exert the will and the power to bring all things under your feet, or all the weaknesses of the flesh under your control. Love is the power I give to you to go forth and fulfill the great destiny for which you were created.

Remember that it is the things of the world which the Gentiles seek, or those who are not inheritors of My Kingdom. Remember that they also love their friends, but HATE THEIR ENEMIES! Of you it is required to forgive all men. Of you it is required to love and pray for your enemies, not in hyprocritical, self-righteousness, but with all the strength of your souls. And of you it is required that you commit your way unto me, and trust in me with all your hearts.

In fulfilling my laws it is not required that you sacrifice yourselves to those who would continually injure and destroy you. Even I avoided those who would have destroyed me before my time, and those I could not help. Give your strength unto me, not to those who would trample your pearls under their feet and turn again and rend you. Forgive such, love

them, and pass on. Hold no bitterness in your
hearts. Let divine compassion tincture every
thought. Let blessings pour continually from
your hearts and turn unto me in every thought
and let praise and joy and thanks be the pulse-
beat of your being.

CHAPTER VII.

THE SEVEN SENSES

Beautiful, earth-born children, lost in the sensual maze of your five earthly senses, listen while I touch you with the finger of light and open up the doors of your understanding. Your five senses are the gifts of the flesh, and by them your minds are endowed with earthly knowledge and given a comprehension of all the things you have experienced. All information brought into your mortal minds, thus far, has been through your five physical senses, the senses of touch, taste, smell, sight and hearing.

The sixth sense is a subject shied away from as a thing of mystery. This sixth sense is the most easy of all to comprehend for it is but the power to think. It is actually the sense of "thinking". The other five senses are connected with the brain and send their information to it. The sixth sense is located within the brain and is the power of the thinking mind to formulate opinions, to weigh conditions, to measure a situation and to evaluate information.

Taste is in the mouth and also in the nose.

The sense of smell is in the nostrils. Vision is in the eyes while the sense of touch is in the nervous system and is registered in every part of the body. The sixth sense is in the brain and is associated with the power of thought.

Beyond the sixth sense is the seventh. It is the sense of inner feeling, or of intuition. In most it is dormant until comprehended. It can be developed and most certainly should be.

This seventh sense, this sacred sense of intuition is the sense of spiritual touch, or knowing. It is a sensitiveness of being that has the power to contact the spiritual. It is the touch that turns belief into "KNOWING". It is a faculty of the soul that was meant to work in conjunction with the mind. It is most refined and spiritual. The mind itself is the link between the physical and the spiritual in man. This seventh sense has the faculty of actually touching the things that are not registered on any of the other senses. My daughters usually have this seventh sense developed more than my sons, for they, as a rule, are more sensitive and more delicately constituted.

To deny this sense because its functions are not registered on the other six senses is not wise. Each sense has its own function and that which one tastes is not registered on the hearing.

Neither are the things one sees necessarily registered on the smell or touch. Occasionally these senses overlap in their functioning. Taste and smell are very closely related. But each has its own distinct work and power and purpose. Therefore because this seventh sense is not registered on the other five senses does not disprove it. Yea, describe to another the taste of an apple, the smell of a rose, the color of a sunset to him who is blind, the glory of a symphony without the instruments to produce a single note, nor the voice to sing.

This seventh sense is less understood only because it is less developed in most people than are the other senses. And it is true that some senses are more keen in some than in others. Some of your own senses may be more intensely sensitive than others.

The purpose and mission of the senses is to give information which accumulates as experience and knowledge is registered by the sixth sense, upon the brain. For instance, if you get burned you learn by sight to discern what is hot, and by touch what the result of that contact means to you.

The six senses were meant to be the obedient servants of man in his physical existence. However they have not always been the servants but have more often been the rulers. When they are permitted to rule they become tyrants and their function grows out of bounds and becomes what was anciently called sensual. "Mankind, from that day forth became carnal, sensual and devilish." Carnal means worldly. Greed, lust, passions and all animal appetites rule in riotous tryanny and man becomes the slave. Wild thoughts run rampant and uncontrolled, and untold evils are the result. Gluttonous appetites and lusts are developed and one degenerates back to the uncontrolled instincts of the animal.

Because of these negative conditions that have come forth through the uncontrolled senses there have been false teachers who have taught that the senses should be deadened. They have viewed the evils of an over-indulgence in the appetites and the complete enslaving of mankind who indulge in them and assumed that the answer is to destroy them. This should never be considered, for it is an answer that brings naught but dullness and a complete deadening of all the glorious equipment with which man was so graciously endowed. If one abuses these divine gifts they automatically become deadened and less keen in the ability to bring joy in the perfection of Gods surroundings and divine blessings. The senses, should, if possible, be intensified by the joy of thanksgiving. But they should always be understood and in complete control. They were meant to be your servants and through them you may learn to comprehend your surroundings and to fulfill your destiny in singing honor, not in deadened existence.

The precious senses, given so graciously to man, should be more keenly developed, intensified and fully appreciated. Through these sacred senses come all your enjoyments of the great creations of the Almighty. And "Man IS that he might have joy."

Learn to appreciate more fully the beauty your eyes behold in tree and flower and fountain and sky, and in the faces of your fellowmen. Learn to rejoice in the melody of music and in the lilting song of the bird. Learn to be thankful for the pure, wholesome food, not too overspiced nor over-seasoned, but in the Father's gifts of great abundance, and as near as He created them as possible. Learn to rejoice more fully in the fragrance of a flower. Let these five senses become to you the messengers of joy. And "Joy is of the saints, and who can put it on but they alone?" To receive a fullness of joy or "A fullness of God," which has been promised to those who would overcome darkness and become filled with that singing song of gratitude is almost synonymous. This joyous ecstasy of singing gratitude prepares one literally for a "Fullness of God."

Train your minds to think only the most beautiful things possible. Learn to rejoice and let that song of inner rejoicing sing in your souls in eternal gratitude for that song of vibrating joy is my Spirit springing into activity within you. This joy is the contact with that sacred seventh sense, and by the inner song of joyous ecstasy and thankfulness and appreciation that divine sense will be developed.

And now, my dearly beloved, I would reveal to you a new mystery. There are seven colors in the rainbow. There are seven notes in an octave. The eighth color is but the first one repeated again. Your rainbow can be repeated again and again in endless multiple expression as purple blends into indigo and indigo into blue and blue into green and green into yellow and yellow into orange and orange into red and red into purple. And so on. Endlessly. Each color related to those on either side.

So it is with music also. Each tone or note is related to the one above and the one below it. Each note is a link in the eternal melody of sound and harmony even as each color is a link in the prism of painted glory. The next

note above the octave is but the first note of
the following octave.

And now, beloved, another mystery I will reveal. When all the seven colors are gathered
back into the one they become the pure white,
the ONE. And to him who has the ears developed to hear, which few have ever done, he
could hear the seven tones of an octave blended
into one master tone and it would be the great
keynote of all harmony, the chime of the great
undertone of the universe. The vibration of
God! The overtone of pure creation and Life
eternal.

And now, to make it more comprehensible,
when the sixth and seventh senses are developed
one goes into the great stage of all-knowing, or
complete comprehension. It is the state in which
he not only hears music but he also sees it. And
it is registered upon his entire being. He not
only smells the perfume of the flower he sees
it and hears it, for it is but vibration.

Yea, all things are an eternal harmony of
vibration. Some of these vibrations are expressed
on taste, others on touch or smell or hearing,
or sight. Yet do they all belong to the ONE,
which is the faculty of All-knowing. When one
learns to intensify the senses in joyous, loving
gratitude and praise they become the great

ALLNESS of complete comprehension, the state of actually knowing and one is filled with the fullness of God, or the fullness of joy and understanding and power, with a complete knowledge of God. This is Life Eternal!

It is now, therefore, the seventh sense and its power and development which I desire to reveal to you. The brain is an organ of the physical being. It is mortal and of the flesh. Since its servants and helpers and power to operate are the first five senses it is limited completely to physical experiences and physical knowledge, unless it has the seal removed, which has caused it to remain blind. This sixth sense which is the power of thought is from the mortal, physical brain. It comprehends, of itself, only tangible things. But this is not its complete power of functioning. It has the power, when developed, to contact the spiritual. This comes when the power to "believe" is developed, then one need no longer go about in what has always been known as "blindness of mind."

As one begins to love God with all his heart, the mind is touched by that outflowing love and can be transformed from a mere physical organ to one in contact with the divine. Such unsealed minds can be endowed with divine purpose and spiritual functioning and will then find contact with the seventh sense, or inner knowing.

You, my beloved, who have truly sought so that you might begin to fulfill that First and Great Commandment, have begun to touch upon the kingdom of the soul and you have learned that in the very center of your beings is another seat of knowing, more perfect and complete than the physical brain. It is where the voice of conscience dwells. It is where the subconscious mind is situated, that marvelous servant or sense that makes all things possible for you. No one can become proficient in anything unless he gains the aid of that deep subconscious mind that never sleeps, never forgets, never tires and has eternal contact with the very throne of God through the superconscious mind. Learn to become aware of this beautiful "Helper" within. Demand of it assistance when you wish to learn something, master some knowledge, or to remember or recall some forgotten truth. Demand its assistance in whatever endeavor you undertake and it will bring you to a degree of perfect mastery.

Within this subconscious mind is the seventh sense. Within it is the power of mastery over any given task. No one ever learned to walk without its aid. None ever learned to operate a machine proficiently, to type, drive a car or ride a bicycle without its abundant help. No one ever became a great musician or mastered any art or profession without its unsleeping, untiring assistance. It is the sacred "HELPER". Learn to be aware of this divine Helper within and appreciate it, giving thanks for its unwearing help. As your awareness increases you will have contact or use of that divine seventh sense. And by the development of the seventh sense all the senses may be blended into the one Great "All-Knowing and All-power, or the superconscious Mind.

This super-conscious mind is the power that is reached by the pure in heart. It is completely spiritual and is situated in the very top of the head. It was known to Enoch and the wise ones of old, as Mt. Zion. Yea, my servant Isaiah described it in his thirty-fifth chapter and reveals to those of spiritual insight that this is the Zion that all must reach who would behold the face of God. This is the Zion to which my beloved ones among this generation will come, singing their songs of everlasting joy. It is the perfecting of that inner, joyous song of gratitude, thanksgiving and love that bears you to the very realms on high, to the Mount Zion, the pure in heart, or the condition of complete purification of heart. And the wicked can never cross over to it, nor the blind and rebellious, though a fool need not err therein.

All the senses are spiritual, intangible, inexplicable, delicate beyond comprehension though registered upon the physical brain, bringing a comprehension of physical, tangible surroundings. Nevertheless, they are spiritual, as are the sixth and seventh senses, but which also have the power to contact the spiritual.

Intensify those senses by giving thanks to God for every beautiful, tangible gift of creation. Let your eyes drink in the wonders of the heavens, and the beauties of the earth and give praise. Let your ears rejoice in melody and you will begin to hear the symphony of the universe echoed in the joy of your own heart. Let your mind remember that it is a gift of God that reveals to you the vibrating essence of perfume, the taste of luscious fruit, the touch of satin.

Let joy increase within you and ascend to the purification of your hearts, the Zion of your own existence, with songs of everlasting joy.

Everything in the universe, in the world and in scripture is symbolical of the things, conditions and powers right within you, my dearlv beloved.

Chapter VIII.

THE POWER OF WORDS

EVERY LETTER in your alphabet, like every key on the piano, has its own vibration. The Alpha and Omega, or the "A" and the "Z", or the Beginning and the Ending is My Title. That "A" and "Z", or Beginning and End is also the symbol of man's journey from the throne of Light out in its great circle of development and progress back again to that throne of Eternal Light, glorified and endowed with knowledge and infinite power. It is the Great Amen.

And every word is also a symbol. The written symbol or the spoken symbol are but a witness of the power behind the word.

Words can become winged messengers of power when released by that inner understanding. No word should ever be wasted. Words are clothed with power when sent forth under strict control, or under great wrath. In either case they go forth with the power of their fulfillment contained within them.

Harsh, angry words are two-edged swords for whatever word is sent forth in blasphemy, wrath or viciousness or unclean words of vile speech will help to disintegrate the very cells of the body and produces a degeneracy of mind, body and soul. Their defiling influences debase the mind, giving the sensual powers the keys of control and one becomes no better than the animals, for he is considered "sub-mortal", or below human.

It is the thinking and feeling behind evil words that bring the full inflow of retribution. Yea, angry words are deadly in their destructive force when hurled forth under intense wrath or hate.

Every vibration, when born of thought and emotion, produces a re-action in the universe that is immeasurable. Only from this higher realm can the force of such vibrations be comprehended.

When these great emotions are clothed with sound, which makes them tangible even to mortal senses, their power is increased an hundredfold.

You speak truth when you express a woman's envy or dislike in such words, as: "She looked daggers at me!" Yea, it is quite so. You can ward off these daggers only by sending out love and compassion. Also are spoken these words: "If looks could kill—". Looks can kill. Looks can be very deadly if behind them is a thought and emotion that is filled with an evil passion, hate, jealousy, fear or malice. But know this, my children, the destructive force is released first in and through the sender's being. It is a two-edged sword. One edge smites the wielder and the other his foe.

The vibrations, or entities sent out, endowed with the power of sound, will travel back again upon the inroads over which they go forth, out through the eyes, the voice, the heart, the fist, the cells and fibres, and returning lodge in the living tissues of the sender, to bring their warring discord into every cell, muscle, nerve and structure of his own body, to distintegrate and destroy.

Yea, looks can kill. But know always that evil is born as a two-edged sword and bears the burden of its going forth. For both the sender and the receiver are jarred and injured by the impact of the destructive vibrations unless the recipient's understanding is enlarged to combat such violence.

"Love your enemies. Pray for those who despitefully use you and persecute you." And know fully and truly that the powers to be forgiven are contained in your own divine power to forgive. This power within you is one of your great

God-given attributes. When it is developed and used you will know that you are beginning to fulfill the command to become perfect.

My lovely children, a sneer is deadly in its sting. Its venom can be more poisonous than the sting of the adder. In a sneer are the vibrations of belittling contempt that can literally slay an individual's confidence in every worthwhile thing, himself, his fellowmen and God. A sneer also is a two-edged sword. First through the sender's face it must go to bring a shadow and the promise of its retributive forces that will return, and the lingering ugliness of its fulfilled promise to become permanent in future days.

There is no law to protect the sender from that which he releases in thought, word or feeling. Those vibrations are his own, borne of himself, and he will become them as they return unto him, multiplied. There is only one way by which he can be spared from their returning vengeance and that is by an immediate repentance. By an awareness of his misdirected, uncontrolled, destructive, evil thought or word or sneer he has the power to send forth speedy messengers of love and light to overtake the bearer of his ills, and thus recalling them, or transforming them, the entities of error and destruction can lose their power or be completely transformed, or converted. Such is the power of the sender.

For the receiver there is always a way of escape. He has but to keep himself clothed in love. If the hate-filled vibrations of another reach him, clothed in this divine armour of Christ, or Light, they are immediately deflected and can do no harm whatsoever. These vibrations, or entities will be instantly transformed into Light upon this contact and will be reflected back with added force to the sender, which, if he will accept can bring healing to him in all its infinite power. Such is your power to heal, my beloved ones. Yea, let this love go forth from you to help bind up the wounds and to heal the evils and the discords and hates of a world.

As your love transforms the messengers of darkness into powers of light they will return to him who released them as blessings, that he might be forever healed. If, however, he rejects this light you return to him in love, then will his transgression be doubled and he will more speedily destroy himself.

Your concern is not whether he accepts these converted, glorified entities you return to him. That is entirely between the sender and God.

Your one and only concern is to see to it that
from you returns nothing but love, compassion,
infinite mercy and forgiveness. In other words,
you are to pray for him with all that great power of forgiving love which is yours to purify,
develop and bring forth. Every opportunity such
as the wrath or hate of a neighbor is an opportunity to perfect yourselves in loving and
forgiving.

Remember your responsibility, my beloved,
as you travel these crowded highways of destruction as they seethe in impatience and tur-
bulent confusion. He who shouts at you or sends
his daggers of discord at you, needs the immediate outpouring of your love. Forgive him
instantly and return his vibrations to him as
divine messengers of love and light. His very
life may be thus held in your hands. For it is
in your power to help stop the great slaughter
along your busy, crowded thoroughfares. Yea,
begin to comprehend and use the divine powers
with which you are endowed and feel them increase within you.

Know also the power of your spoken words.
No word should ever be spoken in wrath, irrita-
tion or at random. Chatter is a waste of the infinite powers of the universe. Yea, beloved, "Let
your minds and lips lose their power to hurt

and wound, and then shall your voices truly be heard among the gods." Let naught but love go forth from you that the great, divine healing might come, first to yourselves, then reach out to heal and bless your associates, and on out to the whole world. It is through you, my children, that the healing must come.

Yea, there is no law to protect the sender from the effects of his evil except his own instantaneous repentance or his acceptance of your forgiving love.

The Hopi Indians, who in past years, through deep trouble and anguish learned to use this power of surrounding themselves with light, though they understood it not nor comprehended the how or why of its reality. But using the power, they can draw, what appears to be an imaginary line, over which none can cross, except in love. They but draw upon their own inner forces to establish a barrier that is stronger than steel.

There need be no "mist-tree" concerning this power, which is yours to use.

Each of you, my beloved, has untold power being unused, mis-used or abused. Let this not be, but learn to walk with me in divine majesty. Yea, within yourselves is the power of contact with the infinite forces of Almighty God, our

Father, power to transform you into masters of Light and love. Yea, there is power to subdue the earth and all the evil conditions upon it, power to touch eternity and play new melodies upon the stars.

Harsh, metallic voices are voices that have never breathed love into their words, never found contact with that inner source of Light, never vibrated with the unspeakable glory of compassion and forgiving, never touched upon the kingdom of their souls, though they may have thought they were serving me all the days of their lives. Yea, and often the service of such has been rendered in bigotry and self-righteousness with naught but condemnation for all who did not agree with them and their own brand of life. Service without compassionate love and mercy is of no value, either to me or to my children.

Power and blessings follow naught but the the service of loving forgiveness, infinite compassion, divine mercy and love such as God holds. Give this caliber of service and you will begin to walk with God. His powers will become your powers, and in your hands will be the blessings that will help restore and glorify the earth on which you dwell.

CHAPTER IX.

THE FRUIT OF THE TREE OF LIFE

THE FRUIT of the Tree of Life is the Love of God that is shed forth in the hearts of the children of men." This is true, my dearly beloved. And those who prefer to think of the Tree of Life as some great Tree surrounded in "mist", making it a "Mist-tree" will have great difficulty in partaking of the Fruit thereof.

To you, my beloved ones, is the power to become branches of this glorious Tree of Life as you permit this Christ love to pour out through you. Yea, you become bearers of the Fruit of the Tree of Life. For I Am the Vine, and you are the branches. I Am the Living Vine, or source from which this infinite love pours out through you, in loving thoughts, loving words and loving acts.

Services in some church or lodge have no comparison to the great service given to a world in this great out-pouring of God's love, through you. In the bringing forth of this love is the fulfilling of all the commandments. Yea, it is

the Fruit of the Tree of Life that will bring
the healing to the nations. It will heal first you
who become the bearers of its Fruit, then your
associates, who will receive of it, through you;
and going on out it will begin to heal your own
nation and then the world on which you dwell.

Yea, my children, this great love of God that
is poured forth through your opened hearts is
truly the Fruit of the Tree of Life. When you
comprehend its power and its reality there will
be no Cherubim, nor flaming sword, to guard
its way, for you, having overcome your sins, will
receive of its fullness. And nevermore will you
hunger and thirst for in it is the power and
fullness of Life. Yea, let your hearts be opened
and your spirits become contrite that it might
find its power of fruitage in you.

Resist not your sorrows, your troubles, your
difficulties and afflictions, but learn obedience
by them for such is the purpose and power of
your sufferings. This is the pruning that must
be given until all that is dead and unproductive
in you is trimmed away by our Father, Who
is the Husbandman.

Relax and release your broken hearts to the
inflowing, outflowing power of love and with
your inner spirits contrite with your many failures you will learn the perfection of my healing

love and the power of my Holy Will. Know this, beloved, contained within my Divine Will is the perfect, glorious perfection of all your divine powers of complete and utter fulfillment of glory and achievement and happiness and fullness of joy.

My Will is never contrary to your will. It is your will that has been contrary to My Will. In My Will is the divine perfection of all that you could hope for, or imagine. Yea, even your own complete pattern of perfection and all the powers thereof.

Yea, bring to me your broken hearts of failures, of shattered dreams, of suffering and error, and with your spirits grown contrite, the "self" in you will be forever lost and you will find your own great inner Self, the ruler of your Kingdom, yea, your own soul. When you have mastered the flesh you will find your own great master, the power of Christ within, and you will become one with it, ever beautiful, ever perfect, ever loving and glorious. This is the pattern of your fulfillment, your own perfection in all things which will answer all your needs. This is what you have unconsciously hungered and thirsted for. This is the fullness of the Tree of Life bearing its perfected fruit through you, the perfecting of love within your own beings.

[89]

Yea, my beloved, be ye bearers of the Fruit of the Tree of Life and let your healing come. And know that this divine Love is shed forth through the Christ center within each one of you. It is that very heart center of your beings that must be opened to its inflow, yea, through your own opened, or broken hearts. Know that it is this contact from within that allows Me to be the Vine and you to become the living branches of glory to bear the Fruit of Life, for the healing of the nations.

It is only when you contact this inner center of Light, or the Vine in your own beings that you can contact the source of Life. This contact is with that "Still Small Voice" within which whispers its wise council in penetrating warmth from the innermost depths of your own beings. This is the contact with the Source of Life. This is the only possible way to become Living Branches of the Tree of Life, with Me as the Vine. This is the only way you can become a fountain for the Living Waters.

These great truths have been presented in many, many ways down the ages, that the great powers behind the words might begin to penetrate your outer consciousness. Nevertheless the blindness of men's minds has been so clouded with the darkness of unbelief that very little of the great Truth has penetrated into man's consciousness.

The Great Day is dawning, my beloved children, and it is time for you to awaken from your deep sleep and comprehend the Truth that you might be free, yea, free from the darkness, the lethargy, the suffering and distress which the great ignorance has caused. Yea, that you might be free and step out into the Light leaving the great darkness behind with its hates, and discords and intense suffering.

Know, my children, my dearly beloved, that when you begin to comprehend the words I spake long ago, and know literally that I Am the Vine and you are the branches that the great Life of Love might begin to pour through you, that your labors be not misdirected nor in vain, you will begin to step forth again in your divine, pristine glory. You will no longer be dead branches, bringing forth your barren sterility and dead works to wither and fall to the earth. Instead you will become a living branch, bringing forth the very Fruit of the Tree of Life. To be a bearer of that divine, All-powerful love with its all-healing, all restoring power of everlasting life. This is the power to KNOW God. It is Life Eternal.

Beloved, when you become the bearer of the

Fruit of the Tree of Life it will no longer matter what you do, or where you serve, for every thought, every word and act will be in tune with the whole universe and fraught with infinite power. Yea, you will become a living benediction to the world whether you contact thousands or dozens, or only a few. Yea, your hands will be filled with the sacred gifts of the Spirit. In your heart will be the song of the universe, the great New Song, winging its way to the very throne of God in songs of everlasting praise and it will heal all things that it touches. Through your being will pour forth the Love of God to help heal and bless a world. And through you shall the healing Fruit of the sacred Tree of Life be offered again to the world. This is the fruit that will heal the nations. And they will be healed of their sickness, their greed for power, their misery and suffering—and death. For I Am the Vine and you are the branches through which this Fruit must be borne.

Chapter X

PRAYER

What is prayer, you ask?

My beloved, prayer is the reaching out of your hand to find that divine contact of power with Me.

Your prayers may be blundering, harmful, selfish petitions, which, if fulfilled according to your asking would hold you back in your progress for many years, or even centuries. Nevertheless prayers are always answered. If, however, they are tinctured, even slightly with the thought, "Of Thy Will Be Done," they can return to you with blessings pure and undefiled.

Prayers can be meaningless, lifeless, habitual mutterings which go no higher than your ceilings and from that level they will be answered. They may be very selfish and harmful and for your injury, or even the injury of others. For instance, like the prayer of an individual praying for the love of someone who does not belong to him, or her. Whereas, if the desire was relinquished to the Will of God that individual might find his, or her own mate within a short time and perfect happiness would follow. Yea, beloved, the harm of all selfish prayers could be healed if you would but relinquish your wills to the Will of God.

There are many prayers that shriek out in anquished despair, praying that two and two will not make four. These prayers that beg for God's laws to be set aside or changed for the gratification of one's lusts, greeds or wicked ways of selfishness are vain and childish prayers. But even then, such prayers are heard. And they are answered, but always in His way.

Know this, my children, "God cannot look upon sin with the least degree of allowance." When you pray for your sins to be made beautiful and for God to change His laws to suit your lusts and glorify your sins, you are actually mocking God and His divine laws which were all given for your own glory and progress. When prayers are offered in order to glorify sin they are in vain. Yea, you are taking His Name in Vain, and will not be held guiltless.

Again I repeat, "God cannot look upon sin with the least degree of allowance." And now I shall explain why. Every law, every divine suggestion, every precious command of our Father was made to map your road to glory. It

is your own pathway back into His presence,
crowned with the complete perfection of your
own divine fulfillment. None of these sacred
commandments are for God's glory. They are
for yours. God does not even need your devotion, nor your tribute, nor your love. But you
need to give such offerings to open up your
souls to His divine love and Light. Yea, you are
the ones who need to give such tribute as he
has asked, such love, such devotion as is required that in such giving your soul might be
purified. If you wish your road to be made easy
give all that is required and then double it, if
possible. When you have fulfilled ALL the laws
—and kept *all* the commandments, then you
will reach the point where the First and Second
Great and Wonderful Commandments will have
to be fulfilled in you, or vice-versa. If you love
God with all your heart you automatically will
obey His every command, with pleasure, for
they will be a joy unto you and not a burden.
The laws He gave are your own glory.

For this reason no sin is allowed for it is but
a block to your own path and will not allow
you to proceed in your journey back into the
Light. As long as you desire your sin more than
you desire to fulfill the laws of God, which are
the eternal laws of your own progress, just so

long will your own progress and happiness be stopped.

For this reason God cannot look upon sin with the least degree of allowance, for it is not allowed on the highway that leads into the great Light. You cannot go and stay at the same time any more than you can serve both God and mammon. The choice is yours and no others. When you desire to serve God more than anything else, when you love Him with all your heart, soul, mind and strength then sin becomes easy to leave behind. It becomes abhorrent to you and you want no part of it. It is no longer a struggle to overcome it, but a glorious, triumphant letting-go.

God cannot look upon sin with the least degree of allowance for it is not allowed upon the pathway that leads back into His presence. He may look upon the sinner with compassion and when that individual sees the error of his ways and seeks forgiveness, and help to overcome, then he can be again enfolded in His healing mercy. Nevertheless the time lost while sin blocked the way may never be regained.

Earnest prayer, tinctured with "Thy Will Be Done" helps to open the door to His very throne. But prayers must be sincere, not groveling petitions to influence God to obey man's will, or to alter His laws, to change His ways or to accept sin and stamp it with His divine approval. And though He may look upon the sinner with compassion the sin remains a sin and all the praying possible will not change the sin. The praying must change the sinner, not the sin.

When the sinner can offer up his broken heart of failures and mistakes and learn obedience by his suffering, and when his spirit becomes contrite and teachable, then will the great healing come. But even then, the healing can only come to the one who committed the sin. The transgression cannot be healed. The sin, and every desire for it must be overcome and cast out. This is true repentance, which is the everlasting, glorious, divine gift of God. And were it not for this gift none could ever return back into His presence, for all have sinned.

For every prayer there is a level. The caliber of the prayer decides the level on which it will be heard, and answered. "His prayers went no higher than the ceiling," is a true saying. And from that level will be sent the answer to the petition which was not filled with enough faith, love or Light to go higher. Such a prayer is not clothed in glory. It went out empty and of low quality. It will return, but its return will not hold the power of the Celestial realms.

[97]

No man is greater than his power of prayer. This does not mean his ability to give great prayers to be heard of men, sent out in deep, sanctimonious tones. Great prayers measure the depth of a man's feeling, the fibre of his soul, the unselfishness of heart, his love for God. The power of prayer is in accordance with the individual's contact with that inner Source of Love and Light in the very depth of his own being.

Yea, from every level your prayers ascend, and on the level of their release will their answer return.

Prayer is not necessarily a thing of words, though words may clothe it with added power.

True prayer is: "The soul's sincere desire, uttered, or unexpressed."

Prayer is not just a petition of the lips. For if "One draws near to Him with his lips, while his heart is far from Him, it is accounted as wickedness. Nor is prayer just a selfish wish of the mind. Any prayer that is offered without feeling has no value whatsoever. And it is true that "The prayers of the Saints come up as incense before the Lord." It is their power of prayer that makes them Saints, for he who can pray with all the energy of heart, or "ask in the spirit" asketh according to the will of God and it will ascend as incense. But incense is but a dead lifeless substance until lighted by the living flames of fire which releases its essence and its power. So is prayer but a lifeless waste unless it is released through the great forces contained within the very depths of your own soul.

Such prayers released by that inner flame of devotion ascend and with their ascension they lift the sender and in his praying the self is forgotten and his soul finds its way to the very throne of God. To such all gates are opened and the powers of heaven hasten to give ear, and to fulfill. Such prayers rise above the selfish little personal desires of one's petty life. Yea, they take on immortality.

Yea, beloved, give heed unto my words that you may learn to reach the very ear of God. All prayers are answered. But all prayers are not noble, nor great, nor filled with good.

During World War One the German soldiers continually prayed, "Gott Mit Us!" It was a vain prayer for the power of God is never with the aggressor who wishes to subdue others for personal, selfish or greedy gains, nor for power. Nevertheless for those who offered this prayer sincerely and with deep devotion there was succor and help for them whether they lived or died. Or lost.

Every prayer that is offered from that innermost center of one's being is filled with ineffable power and ascends on the very wings of Light. Such prayers outgrow all selfish aims and personal lust and within them is contained the power to lift not only the individual, but a world. Such prayers can fulfill your complete surrender to the Will of God wherein all power and glory lies, even the perfection of your own precious fulfillment.

And now, I speak new words to you, words that hold meanings as yet unknown. Prayer, when released from the center of your soul is not an anguished cry of listed wants and petty yearnings, nor of hopeless despair, nor moanings and weepings, nor of desperate pleadings. Prayer, which rises from the center of your soul is a song of praise and ecstasy and thanksgiving. When you pray from the very center of your soul the powers of heaven are contacted and their joy and power released to vibrate in that great dynamic song of glory upon the very stars. Thus all power is released to blend with the perfect will of God, which is the complete fulfillment of all perfection, or will lead to it that it might be fulfilled in you.

When singing gratitude and thanks and love and praise become the burden of your prayers then will your power mingle with the powers of heaven to help redeem a world.

"And it shall come to pass that he that asketh in Spirit shall receive in Spirit.

"He that asketh in Spirit asketh according to the will of God, wherefore it is done even as he asketh.

"And again, I say unto you, all things must be done in the name of Christ, whatsoever you do in the Spirit.

"And ye must give thanks unto God in the Spirit for whatsoever blessings ye are blessed with."

Let your prayers of thanks become symphonies of selfless gratitude and praise and they will reach the HIGHEST without delay and from the highest realm will come the fulfillment of thy joy.

Devoted prayers of selflessness have been needed since time began. There have been so few who have ever reached this height of love and understanding so as to become one with the very mind and Will of God and with eyes completely single to His glory. Those who have attained this height are they whom I have reserved unto myself, and they have become clothed in Light, literally.

Many times in days and years gone by, Holy Angels have been sent to comb the earth in search of earnest, unselfish prayer, and finding none, have returned to weep before the throne of God. There have been many anguished prayers, pleading for loved ones, for personal friends, personal desires and wants and they have been answered, or will be in due time. But prayers which concern just oneself or one's loved ones and personal friends is not enough to help purify the earth and produce the balance of power necessary to save it from the forces of evil and of darkness.

Yea, "Put on the whole armor of God, that ye may be able to stand against the wiles of the devil. For we wrestle not against flesh and blood, but against principalities, against powers, against the rulers of darkness of this world, against spiritual wickedness in high places."

Sometimes but one person has been found upon the earth with the power of prayer purified to such an extent it could avert the destruction of the world.

During the Spanish Inquisition such powers were released by twelve-year old Johan Pajares, who stood bound to the stake with the flames

of fire consuming his body. His father stood
beside the boy also giving his life to the flames
for having dared to read the Bible. But the grief
of the father over the sacrifice of his young son
was so mingled with anguish, despair and bitterness over the burning of Johan that it did not
ascend in its purity and power. It was small
Johan who lifted his eyes to heaven and thanked
God that he could give his life, with his father's,
that he could give his life for God, and these
words rose to his lips and reached out beyond
the flames, beyond the world, beyond the skies:
"Dear God, in the name of Jesus, let our lives
open up the way for all men to be permitted to
read Thy Holy Word, from now on and forever." It was the power of Johan's prayer that
was used to end the darkness behind the Inquisition.

Again, such a one kneeled alone in his dungeon during the French Revolution, when
France was reaping the retribution of evil and
darkness for having slain my Saint, Joan of Arc.
And in that retribution blood ran in rivers, and
love was not as hate and fear roared forth in
screaming waves to overwhelm and submerge
the race of men.

Above the tumult and the thunder and the
cry of hate and suffering arose the prayer of a

gray-haired man who had seen his family slaughtered en masse, and knew his own time was near at hand. And kneeling in his dungeon cell, he prayed a prayer that could be used to end the strife, the slaughter and the madness. It was a prayer of infinite love of divine forgiveness and of selflessness and complete surrender.

"Into your arms, Almighty Father, I give my family, and my every friend, for they have all been slain. They have been killed, Holy Father, for no sin save the desire to live true to their nobility, which all men are endowed with, yet know it not. And now, Oh God, I kneel upon the altar of Thy guillotine to give my life, that from my offering peace might come. Yea, as I give my life freely, and with infinite love I pray that it might be used to end this flood of madness.

"Dear God, let those whose hands are drenched with the blood of the innocent see the horror of their acts, that this endless slaughter might be stayed. And then, Dear God, forgive them and hold them not accountable for their sins. Forgive them, God, and let my blood help atone for the carnage that has covered this beautiful land. Yea, let not the taking of my life be in vain, nor held to their charge. But Father, in the name of Jesus, let it be for thy eternal glory.

Let it help to lift the curse from this benighted land that Thy healing might descend and sanity reign once more—Amen."

Two days later, as Louis Beauvais kneeled with his head bowed to receive that final stroke that would sever life, there was a song of glory singing in his soul as the Holy Spirit of Promise bore witness to his soul that his prayer would be fulfilled and his offering accepted.

Within a week the great slaughter of France subsided and the healing commenced. It was the strength of Louis Beauvais' prayer that gave the power to turn the tide of destruction and brought sanity out of the chaos and slaughter.

Again, a few years hence, so close it was but yesterday, the earth was combed to find the power of a true prayer, a prayer with strength to stem the tide of war and bring a temporary peace upon this anguished world. This time it was found in the heart of a little girl who lay crushed and half-buried beneath a mass of stone which, but a few hours before had been the housing place of pride and arrogance.

Captain Yerma and his soldiers were working frantically to release the body of his little sister, Naneia, whom all loved. As they worked, Naneia's ear, pressed against the earth, heard the tread of marching feet.

"Go! Go, my brother! Take your men and hide in these ruined buildings, that you might survive, to fight again for I hear the marching of many feet!"

"And leave you here to die, my little Naneia? Oh, No!"

"If you do not go you will all die in vain. Then there will be none to fight. Let me die for the rest of you. God wants it so! Please, my brother, grant that I do not die in vain. Nor the rest of you. I will surely die anyway but it will be in vain unless it spare you and your soldiers."

Her pleading was so ardent and so sincere that the small army hid themselves according to her urging. Then she bit her lips to hold back the cry of pain so that the invaders would pass her by unseen. Then from her heart arose a prayer so intense she forgot her pain and suffering as she pleaded for God to end the war and spare those whom she loved, and the whole world. It was a prayer that completely detached Naneia from her pain and from the hurt—and from her body. It was the power needed to turn the tide of battle and evict the enemies of her native land, the prayer that paved the way for peace.

Today is the first time in many, many years

when the Spirit of true prayer is beginning to ascend from the earth with enough power and unselfishness to reach out and convert and transmute the very forces of darkness.

Oh, my dearly beloved, forget your personal desires, forget the self, forget your own individual misfortunes and wants, and kneel with me, that in your offering there might be the power to bring the great healing, yea the fulness of the great Light. Offer yourselves and your prayers upon the altar of complete surrender. And if you can find the greatness within to offer your very souls, if necessary, for the redemption of the world, it will not be in vain. Yea, offer up your will to Me. Give me your all. If you can be big enough, in your complete surrender, it will help to bring the rending of the veil of darkness by transmuting it into Light.

I tell you this, beloved, that you might comprehend the complete surrender of the "self" and become a messenger of Light and have the power to help rend the veil of darkness from the earth. And with this glorified prayer I must suggest that you give up every personal desire and concern for yourself, your own perfection, even your desires of fulfilling. Give the self, your life, your mind in a joy of loving, singing devotion that will banish the darkness. Yea, "Turn unto me in every thought." Only in this way can you work with me to bring to pass that which is to come.

Prayer is the greatest power in existence. Prayers are always heard, and answered. "Ask and ye shall receive, seek and ye shall find; knock and it shall be opened unto you; for such is the eternal promise of heaven." But beyond the asking, the seeking and the knocking is the prayer of power that will reveal the very throne of God. This is the prayer of joyous thanksgiving, of loving devotion, of eternal praise. Yea, let your prayers of praise and glory and gratitude and singing ecstasy ascend unto the throne of God and e'er long you will ascend with them to praise before His throne day and night, which is the promise of a fulness of joy which is to sing forever in every cell of your beings in the New Song of praising glory.

Chapter XI.

"BORN OF THE SPIRIT"

In order to command legions one must first be able to command himself, for "He who ruleth himself is greater than he who rules kingdoms."

To be born of the Spirit is one thing, to go on after this Spiritual birth, even to full maturity, is quite another. To reach the full maturity of the Spirit it is quite necessary to continue to hunger and thirst after righteousness.

This maturity comes, beloved, as you learn to continue in steadfast prayer and rejoicing. Then will hope turn into abundant faith, and faith becomes knowledge endowed with power. Never cease to hunger and thirst until you receive the very "Fullness of God." This inner perfection which must be brought forth until it fills all the outer realm of your being and life is the completion of your divine destiny as far as this sphere of action is concerned. For know this, my greatly beloved, that you cannot bring this inner perfection of complete selflessness and devotion into full activity without changing the conditions around you and in the lives of others. This is done by *living* the higher laws of righteousness, not just by believing them. "Even the devils believe."

Understand, beloved, that after one is born he must develop into full maturity. To be born of the Spirit but places you upon the road of spiritual progress which only ends with the very "FULLNESS OF THE FATHER." Then, and then only has the soul developed to its full stature and the spiritual birth fulfills its measured requirement.

This being "born again" is a principle upon which millions have placed their hope of salvation. And they know not that "salvation" is but the infant state of immaturity. It is but the state of a new-born child.

It is for those who continue on the upward path after their infant feet have been placed upon the sacred highway of Light, who continue the inner striving to find, and to know God, who continue to develop into the fullness of maturity, to whom all powers are given. These are they who learn to hear My Voice, to fulfill the Will of God, to keep His Commandments with a glory of singing joy. Each commandment, each suggestion of the Father is but a way-mark along the glorified path of exaltation. For such as continue to follow his commands with joy there shall come the time of contact from within and His Living Life-Giving Words will become a part of life itself. For such the tests of actually knowing God become a glory and not a burden, a joy and not a sorrow, an opportunity and not a punishment, for one must be tested and tried in all things in order to rise above all things.

Salvation is for the weak, for those who never stand upon their own feet, who never learn to walk with God, in their own strength. Salvation is for those who lean on their appointed leaders, or on the strength of others. These are they who let others do their thinking and who never waken their souls for that divine hungering and thirsting to actually know God, that they might walk with Him. These are the ones who can be lulled to sleep in a crib that is too short for growth and with a covering too narrow for the great spiritual covering required for full maturity.

Salvation is My Gift to all. It is my gift to every human being who does not forfeit his right to it. In the love of my sacrifice of Myself was contained the power of your salvation if you will only accept it. It was, and is, given freely. It is for all except those who forfeit it by transgressions too great to be forgiven, or by a rejection that is filled with complete knowledge. Salvation is for those who only accept "Being born again" or "Being born of the Spirit" as the complete fulfillment and goal of all righteousness and the end of the struggle, instead of only the beginning. It is for those who permit others to do their thinking and who never learn to walk in their own greatness, fulfilling their own complete destiny and pattern of life.

Yea, beloved "salvation" is the infant's reward. It is for those who failed to mature to the "Fulness of the Father", in a love and selflessness and joyous devotion that surpasses and by-passes the tears and anguish and darkness and selfish desires and petty petitions and steps into a love that disdains rewards and personal glory. It is a love so perfect it has eyes only single to the glory of God, and with such a love a full maturity of the soul is completed. Thus the glory of God, as you seek to fulfill it, becomes your glory and your fulfillment.

Yea, my dearly beloved, exaltation is for those who fulfill their own promise of greatness by leaving the "self" behind. These are they who reach their full maturity of soul and learn the power of walking with God. These are they who develop the power to rend the veil of dark-

ness, first within themselves, then reaching out
they help to rend it from the face of the earth.
By the development of perfect love, by thanksgiving and joyous ecstasy they become united
with the very power of eternal Light.

To shout 'Hallelujah' is not enough. To be
good is not enough. To live as the professing
race of Christians have lived during the last two
thousand years IS NOT ENOUGH! Neither is
it enough to give every moment of your life to
fill some high position. Such positions usually
are the complete reward for such service as one
is lifted in prestige and receiving the coveted
honors of men.

The great reward, the complete fullness, the
divine maturity which must fulfill the purpose
of "being born of the Spirit" is the overcoming
of the physical self. This little mortal "self",
willed with its self-important ego must step a-
side to let the soul progress into its destined,
complete, glorified maturity. It is the awakening of the soul that holds the "Spiritual birth".
It is the development of the soul to its full maturity that holds the fullness of God. It is the
little mortal self with its prides, its lusts, its
weaknesses and faults and fears and burdens of
accumulated darkness that is blocking the progress of the soul. It is the self-righteousness of

man that is holding back the New Day even more than the wickedness of defiance and rebellion.

The full maturity, which is meant to follow the birth, or awakening of the soul, can only come after one has overcome the little mortal self. As long as this outer, physical being predominates and rules, one is serving mammon, or the flesh. When the spirit rises up to the equal of the physical, begins to give battle for its heritage as the "first-born" to the throne, or rulership, then the victory can be achieved and the rightful heir to the throne can begin its righteous rule. This struggle is one that is completely unobserved by the outside world. And he who boasts of it and of his progress, or even mentions his degree of salvation is still in the infant state.

Remember, beloved, that the Spirit is the "first-born" for it was born, or clothed in Spirit form long before the physical birth. It is the "first-born" and is heir to the rulership of the body and its senses. When the rightful heir to the throne of your own being takes over all things are completed and fulfilled for it is a rule of power and love and perfection and glorified achievement.

My beloved, when the praises and honors of

men can become of no consequence to you, when you no longer feast on the soft flatteries of men, when the high seats have lost their glamour and cease to feed the lust of pride, and when all evil thoughts and desires for rewards have been completely put aside and you are delighted to take the "least seat" and become "the least", then you are near your maturity. That is how one becomes "the least". It is the overcoming of the little mortal self. Then can you become the "greatest" for then the Spiritual takes over and all things will be fulfilled in you. As you become the greatest all things will become subjected unto you, both in heaven and on earth, the Life and the Light, the Spirit and the Power, sent forth by the Father, through Me, Jesus Christ, His Son.

My dearly beloved, when you realize that of your physical self you can do nothing, that your phsical being holds no power, then God can clothe you in "the white raiment" and you will be clothed indeed. Then will the "shame of your nakedness" be covered so that it will never appear and you will realize that I Am the Vine. You will then know that your own works, though they took your entire strength, time, talents and even your life were but dead and empty works. When the pure love of God can be shed forth through your heart, without malice, prejudice, pride or darkness in its forgiving, compassionate, Christ-Like divine essence that you will find yourself clothed in Light, endowed with infinite power, giving out the healing power of eternal love and One with God.

Now, beloved, if you can learn that your own greatness must unfold through the divine Will of God, as you learn to place yourself in complete and utter surrender to His Divine Will, though it be to the cross, you will come into the fullness of your resurrected soul, as the seals to its tomb are removed from within you and it steps forth clothed in the Almighty power of God.

You will then realize that the greatest tragedy the world ever held was my crucifixion, which was also the greatest blessing ever given. Your own crucifixion of "self" upon the cross will bring forth your own resurrection into the great powers of the Almighty Father. When your Will can become one with His Will you will have "the ears to hear" and you will comprehend the music of the spheres and will become a part of the very vibrations and harmony of the divine song of Universal Triumphant glory, the New Song. Yea, then will your heart be opened wide to my pure love as it flows forth, through you, and on out to bind up the broken, to heal the halt, to restore the lame and the blind and bless and redeem the earth upon which you stand. Then will all the great and holy promises that have been made since time began be fulfilled in you. Then will you be able to do the works that I did. And the first work required of me is the same that is required of you, even the overcoming of the little physical, mortal self. This was my struggle, even as it is yours.

After the "self" is overcome then can you go on to do the greater works, for I will be with you. Yea, my beloved, and according to the promise, I will reveal the Father unto you and you will receive of His Fullness, even the complete maturity of your own sacred, divine souls.

Such are my promises and such will be their fulfillment unto you, for the promises cannot be broken, neither can they remain or return unto me unfulfilled.

Yea, beloved, overcome the flesh, with its prides, its lusts, its bigotry and hatefulness and darkness and let the soul begin to develop into its full maturity. And as you commence this journey you shall know that you are walking the path with me, that I am with you. When you have finished it you shall henceforth "walk with God."

CHAPTER XII.

THE GREAT AMEN

Now is the day, my beloved, to look beyond men, to God! Look beyond mortality, beyond its positions, beyond the powerful phraseology of learned discourses into the souls of men, and know that only he is to be heeded whose works bear witness of his power and his contact with God.

Yea, all who have not the full power of my Father's promises made manifest in their lives are still but infants. Or at best they are only small children, for none have matured into the fullness of the Spirit, though they lay claim to the very gates of heaven, or even the throne of God, if they have not perfected the gift of love in their lives and walk in its Light.

Yea, beloved, come to my arms that I might hide the shame of your nakedness and clothe you with the Light of my power, that you might be healed, and made perfect.

And you, my noble and great ones, who hunger and thirst after righteousness, remember that I promised that you should be filled, even with the "Fullness of the Father." No promise is greater than this. The very heavens are rejoicing over you who have continued to ask, to seek and to knock, even according to my commandment and have not been satisfied to sleep in your infant state of immaturity, expecting God to do all things for you. Rather have you sought to perfect yourselves, even as Your Father in heaven is perfect. This perfection is His eternal desire and plan for you.

My servant Paul admonished that you lay hold of the best gifts. And how could you lay hold of them except to ponder them in your minds and to set your hearts upon them. Then having faith in Me, who was their author, open up your hearts to receive their fulfillment. Yea, Paul, through my commandment unto him, admonished that you leave the Gospel of repentance and baptism and the laying on of hands behind, laying not again the foundation of dead works, after they have been complied with and fulfilled, but from there on go on unto perfection.

Yea, beloved, when you have finished with the first grade leave its texts and lessons, and using the knowledge gained, go on to higher grades of development and learning and service. Yea, go on unto perfection.

Most individuals, on joining the church, think they have done all. How could they think otherwise since the churches teach such doctrine and place such seals upon the minds and souls of their members and converts, thus stopping their progress? Beyond the rituals of the churches, beyond their dogmas and forms is the beckoning reality of the greater Life. Reach on through to the reality and linger not behind, playing with the outer symbols of the great, eternal reality. Nay, be ye not eternal children, playing always with your childish blocks. But rather go on to receive all that is possible. Use the alphabetical symbols on the little wooden building blocks as stepping stones into the realm of divine knowledge and living, and eternal truth.

Never be satisfied, beloved, with anything less than I promised. Never be satisfied with less than the full maturity of your own soul. Never be satisfied until you fulfill the great possibility of your own complete destiny and divine calling. Never be satisfied until you have beheld my face, and then go on until you actually KNOW God.

He who knows not God always talks about it. He who knows God does not tell it.

Beloved, as long as you continue to hunger and thirst, to ask, to seek and to knock, the seals upon you cannot become so strong that they can actually stop and damn your progress. If you continue to search and to hunger and thirst after righteousness, not assuming that you have received all, the path of development will continually unfold, if you seek me diligently, in humility and prayer. Yea, seek me diligently and ye shall find me.

Beloved, remember that those who seek for the great fulfillment that they might awe the minds of men, or to receive praise and honors and to fill high places with their presence but search in vain and their struggle will end in disappointment and failure.

To hold high positions, to receive the adulation and honors of men, to exult in the pride of greatness is as vain to the growth of the soul as it is useless to try building an infant body into maturity by rubbing food on the outside. This is not the way of growth.

Growth is always from within, either in the physical, mental or spiritual realms. To bask in the flatteries and praises of men, to walk in that self-superior attitude of "being the Lord's a-nointed", expecting to be appreciated and exalted by such methods is very childish. And those who indulge their inward cravings to this extent are considered but very "spoiled children" from the higher viewpoint. Such cravings for recognition and honor and the basking in positions and receiving credits is vainglorious and not only stops the soul's growth but actually begins to shrivel it.

My dearly beloved, know that as you step beyond the little physical, mortal self with its bigotries, and lusts and insatiable hunger for credit and rewards, into the higher understanding of growth, the body becomes the vehicle through which the progress of your soul is accomplished.

It is through, and IN the body, that all things must be overcome. Open your mind to comprehend the fullness of these words that you may know fully and completely that it is only possible to receive a fullness of joy while the body and spirit are united. Without the body the spirit has nothing with which to overcome.

The spirit is glorified through the body. The body is the crucible in which the spirit is refined. When the spirit is exalted and fully matured it exalts the body to its level and both can be redeemed and glorified together. This is the law I exemplified, the pattern I gave, the law of fulfillment. Life itself is an opportunity to overcome and pass right on into the Spiritual

Kingdom of complete, glorified maturity, which is intended for every child of earth.

Within each soul is engraved a divine and glorious destiny that is so far beyond anything man has, as yet visualized, it is completely overwhelming in its magnitude of glorious perfection. And this fulfillment, this complete growth and glory has to be achieved by, and through the flesh.

The body contains the necessary equipment and conditions the soul requires to overcome.

Overcome what, you ask? Overcome the self, the little mortal, ego-filled self that, in its pride and bigotry and sensual lusts blocks the way to heaven. Yea, overcome the little self that gloats over praise and high positions and the honors of men, the little self that actually believes, in some instances, that it has a monopoly upon God and upon His holy favors and graces, though He proclaimed aloud that He is no respecter of persons, nor positions. He has always selected the weak and foolish ones as his chosen vessels, to confound the learned and the wise. Yea, overcome the little self that seeks its own and only loves its own, and itself. Overcome the little self that seeks to cover or ignore its own weaknesses and sins and failings, while magnifying them in others. Yea, overcome that little mortal self that so violently stands up to give battle in that overcoming.

Beloved ones, despair not. It is the weaknesses in that little physical "self" that serves as the testing ground, or is the battlefield. Yea, beloved, fear not as you step forth and realize that you are the crucible in which the dross is burned away. Yea, the body is the crucible in which your own refinement takes place and through it is the process given that purifies, perfects and glorifies if you will only bear the tests. Yea, truly was it proclaimed anciently in questioning solicitude, "Who can stand the test of knowing God?"

Yea, who can stand the refining, the overcoming, the intense purifying that is needed to be clothed in His Fullness?

Nay, beloved, despair not at the road ahead. Only know that it is a great and glorious privilege to be endowed with a body of flesh through which your soul might overcome, if you will but permit it. Know that every glorious breath is a divine privilege and an opportunity, for as long as you have the breath of life manifest within you, just so long do you have a chance for ultimate victory. Yea, as long as intelligence can function within you and breath lasts there is the power to turn the tide of battle and achieve the great victory. It is the great battle of decision in which you yourselves must make the great decision and achieve eternal victory as the "First-born" begins its reign.

When one leaves this sphere, without his body, in what you call "death" he relinquishes his greatest opportunity of existence. For in the resurrection those who are filthy will be filthy still and those who are unhappy will be unhappy still; and those who are failures will be failures still; and those who are groveling weaklings will be groveling weaklings still, though all were meant to be divine masters and walk in majesty and power.

And it is true that those who were happy shall be happy still, and those who were righteous will be righteous still. But know this, my beloved, that all who die will have to stand before the judgment seat of God and be judged according to the deeds done in the flesh. Yea, they will be brought into judgment. But for those who receive of these higher laws and overcome all things there is no death, nor judgment, for these things will be done away in you. Yea, the last enemy to be overcome is death. Overcome your darkness, your fears and weaknesses and death will have to back down before you. This is my eternal law. It is automatic in its fulfillment. It is the seal that will be placed upon your forehead, the seal of the Father, the seal of maturity and power and overcoming, for you are MINE.

Those who do not wake up their souls enough to give battle for their divine heritage that the rightful heir, even the "first-born", which was the spirit, can take the reigns of government the battle can never be won. It is for the individual to overcome the darkness right within himself, the fears, the negatives of the flesh, otherwise he will carry them across with him into the realm beyond. It is the flesh that provides the equipment for overcoming, the opportunity and power for complete "Exaltation".

Oh Life! Life stupendous, immeasurable, abundant Life!

Yea, beloved, let every breath be a song of fulfillment, a rhythm of praise, an opportunity of exulting in the glorious gifts and opportunities of God. It is this blessed mortal life of yours that unfolds and holds every opportunity of fulfillment, of triumph, of maturing and of stepping across a million years of travel in one short life-span.

Yea, beloved, every heartbeat is an opportunity! Every breath contains the power of your own exaltation. Every thought and feeling is endowed with the powers of creation and complete fulfillment.

Recall, my beloved, my parable of the laborers in my vineyard and those who sat idle in the market place until the last hour? Yea, suppose your life has passed and you have failed to find your place and the powers of your own maturity and fulfillment. This last hour need not be lost if you will but turn to me and offer up your broken hearts of failure and lost years and with your final energy serve in the joy of this last hour.

Know this, beloved, the great growth of the soul is not made in anguished tears of agony, but rather in the joy of praise and the adoration of singing gratitude. For he who is thankful in all things shall be made glorious. Yea, in that inner song of praise and ecstasy and thanksgiving is stored the love divine, the love that casts out all fear, the power to fulfill all things.

And now, another mystery I will reveal unto you. This one is most sacred, see that you cast it not before swine lest they trample it under their feet and turn again and rend you. This most sacred truth which I now reveal unto you is the great Name AMEN. This is the Name through which you seal your prayers and petitions, and is most holy. It is the Title of the

Beginning and the End. It is My Title. **And** it
is yours, when you have fulfilled it. It is **the**
Name which includes all things, your progress
from the time you left the throne of God as rays
of Light, to go on your way of progress to be
clothed in consciousness, then in Spirit form and
at last in flesh as you continue in your round
of progress back again into the very presence
of God, clothed in eternal Light and glory.

When you have completed this round of progress you will have fulfilled the Great Amen,
the promise and fulfillment of your own divine
perfection, the perfect pattern contained within your own soul. Then you shall truly comprehend all things, and all things will be subjected
unto you.

Yea, glory to God our Father! Glory and
honor and praise be unto Him forever and forever—AMEN!

Chapter XIII.

THE UNSPEAKABLE NAME OF JESUS CHRIST

My dearly beloved, let me now teach you the purpose of my sacrament, or the holy communion, for it is indeed the holy communion for those who comprehend its true reality. I shall reveal to you the purpose of the prayer that was intended to establish the ordinance of administering the broken bread, symbol of my broken flesh, or "the self" completely overcome and subdued. My overcoming was portrayed on the cross. So is yours. It will be on the cross of your testing that the little, petty self will be overcome and the greater self, the spiritual self step forth to assume command and to rule in glory. Yea, the broken flesh is but the symbol of the broken, or open heart when the flesh has been overcome. And the wine is but the symbol of the living fountains of eternal life, of which you are invited to partake. It too was symbolized in the shedding of my blood, the emblem of mortal life. This great love, which I offer, is but the great out-pouring essence of the eternal life stream I desire to endow you with. It is the symbol of the Waters of Life. And now I invite you to come and partake of the Waters of Life freely.

Again, I shall give the sacramental prayer as I gave it on that evening of the Feast of the Passover: "Oh God, the Eternal Father, I ask thee to bless and sanctify this bread to the souls of all those who partake of it, that they may eat it in remembrance of my broken body, and witness unto thee, Oh God, the eternal Father, THAT THEY ARE TO TAKE UPON THEM THE NAME OF THY SON, AND ALWAYS REMEMBER ME, THAT THEY MIGHT ALWAYS HAVE MY SPIRIT TO BE WITH THEM—AMEN.

"Jesus Christ" is only the spoken symbol of my name. And in every language, and according to every tongue is the pronunciation different and varied. Behind words that are spoken in many tongues and in as many ways there is the real name, The unspeakable Name, for it can never be spoken. It is beyond language and tongue and physical expression. It is the true and living Name, the Divine Reality.

It is this Great Name which you are required to take upon you as you partake of my Holy Sacrament or Communion. For in this Name is all communion held with Me, and with my Father.

This unspeakable Name contains the living reality of all Life and Light and power, and the fulfilling of the words, "If you ask anything in my Name I will do it." Or "Whatsoever you shall ask in the Name of My Son, Jesus Christ, it shall be done even according to your words."

Beloved, when you ask in that glorious spirit of vibrating ecstasy and gratitude and praise you are asking in My Name, or in the Spirit. Open your hearts that you may comprehend.

"And it shall come to pass that he that asketh in Spirit shall receive in Spirit.

"He that asketh in Spirit asketh according to the will of God, wherefore it is done even as he asketh.

"And again, I say unto you, all things must be done in the Name of Christ, whatsoever you do in the Spirit.

"And ye must give thanks unto God in the Spirit for whatsoever blessings ye are blessed with."

Now, to you, beloved, I shall open up your understanding that you may see and comprehend the meaning behind the holy sacrament, or communion, so that in Spirit we might commune together. It is in and through this holy,

inner communion with me that you can take upon you My Name, not the spoken symbol, but
the living reality of all which the Great Unspeakable Name represents. It is your privilege
and right to take upon you this Name that you
might truly always remember me, according to
your part of the covenant. It is not for my sake
that you must remember me, but for your own.
Yea, that you might fulfill all things, even as I
fulfilled them, and do the works which I did.
Yea, even the works which I fulfilled within
myself must you also fulfill within yourselves,
even the complete overcoming of the "self", not
in tortuous affliction, but rather in joy and praise
and thankfulness and love and devotion and
singing gratitude. Yea, this was the first work
which I did. This is the first work which is required of you. It is how the darkness is overcome and you learn to turn unto me in every
thought, overcoming the "self", the negatives
the darkness and evils through praise and love
and devotion. This was, and is, the meaning
and the pattern of my life. I came into the world
to show you the way that you too might fulfill
even as I fulfilled.

The true order of prayer, as I have told you
in this work, is not a begging attitude, not a
whining monologue of complaints nor distraught

weeping supplications nor lamentations. The true prayer is the opening of the soul, or learning to enter the secret chamber of your own inner being and there holding Holy Communion with Me. In this communion there is no sorrow, no weeping, no despair. There is naught but peace and power and singing glory of such vibrant rejoicing no words can possibly contain it. It is the power beyond words. It is the fulness of that vibrant song of ecstasy which is the symphony of the Universe. It is the New Song, the song that is sung before the throne of God day and night, that song of infinite rejoicing, devotion and eternal praise and love. It is the place where all power lies, or is contacted, where all joy is released and where all faith abides. It is your own access to the very throne of God. It is not a condition of jumping hysteria, nor shouting babble, nor uncontrolled confusion which you receive in this Holy Communion. It is the sublime power of dignified majesty. It is the point of complete control. It is the realm of eternal Light.

Within this inner, Holy Communion you receive the power to take upon you My Name. Not the outer symbol of the spoken word, but the living reality of all It holds within It of majesty and power and fulfilment.

Yea, beloved, learn to hold yourself in this great vibration of Living Light, thus always remembering Me, that you might always have my Spirit, or the Spirit of the Christ Light to be with you. It is in this great inner vibration of singing thanks and love and high rejoicing and praise that My Unspeakable Name of infinite power is held. As you contact It and receive the Waters of Life, and the bread of Life in this divine communion my unspeakable, Living Name will be revealed unto you. It is the Name of All-power. And you shall take upon you that Name. Yea, and you too shall fulfill it, for it will be revealed unto you. Then you, beloved, shall be clothed in my Spirit and receive of my power.

In your hands, beloved, you who have hungered and thirsted after righteousness I am now placing the keys of all fulfillment. And that my promises may not return unto me void and unfulfilled, I am revealing unto you the great mysteries of my Kingdom. And so I say unto you, "Come! Yea, to my beloved the Spirit and the bride say, Come! And let him that heareth say, Come, and let him that is athirst come; and whosoever will, let him take of the waters of life freely."

So be it—AMEN.

Chapter XIV.

"IT IS MORE BLESSED TO GIVE THAN TO RECEIVE"

Beloved, "It is more blessed to give than to receive." The great out-pouring currents of God's pure love is continually being offered to all, but until you open up your heart, that you, in turn might give it out, there is no blessing in it. Your blessing is not in the receiving of this great love. It is always there for you to receive. It is your seeking to give it that brings the blessings and starts the great inflowing, outflowing of its great healing glory. As you give this love it pours out to you and out from you, bringing the healing first to you, then to those whom you love, and then to those who have hated you. It washes away all hates, all discords, all confusion, all lack and imperfection. And the greater your love the more far-reaching it will be and the greater the blessings it will carry upon its wings.

If your love can become great enough and your giving ability expand enough, you can help to bring about the very healing of the nations.

Through this great love the seals within you can be removed, even the hardness of your heart and the blindness of your mind and the other five seals that have held you bound in dismal, unenlightened unprogressiveness while the very realms of Light have held out open gates to you.

Beloved, as you give forth this love you place yourself in tune with the very voice of God. The perfect love is the one perfect gift. And the giver is more benefitted than he who receives.

He who gives, with even the faintest desire of receiving favors, is giving for show and for reward and his gift will be as unproductive as though he gave not. Such giving is not acceptable and it is barren of love, seeking only reward. Therefore in thy giving, give with all your heart. Do not even expect appreciation, for appreciation is the poorest pay possible to receive. Appreciation too often brings a "beholding" attitude which can be turned instantly into resentment. For this reason it is best to give freely, without hope of reward or appreciation.

Give love, and let not thy words proclaim thy giving unless thou art directed to thus express it in words.

Yea, pour out thy gift of love without hope or reward or of compensation or credit. Give love to the weak and the humble, to the lost and the sinner, to the saint and to thy friends. And give a double portion to thine enemies for they are more in need of the healing balm than others. The Pharisees of old loved their own. They loved their friends, but hated their enemies. Of you, beloved, it is required that you love your enemies so that your enemies might be converted by thy love and made into thy friends, that you might be one, in Me. And as you give this pure, divine love of Christ (of Light), with its forgiving mercy you will be forgiven, for it holds the power of your own forgiveness.

Yea, let thy love flow out to thine own. Then let it flow out beyond thine own to all who exist, for they are God's own. And they too need to be healed and reclaimed through love. And in the giving of this great love you will know that it is more blessed to give than to receive, for in the giving you receive double.

Every human being is hungry for love, though few have learned to bestow it. Parents love their children, and often show it only by giving worldly gifts, which the parents desire their children to have, or which their children request or demand. Often the child does not desire the gift the parents give and where there is no desire there is no appreciation or joy in receiving. Gifts, to be fully enjoyed, must first be desired. "Ask and you shall receive, seek and you shall find, knock and it shall be opened unto you," is wisdom beyond mortal comprehension.

Beloved, know this, no gift is so greatly needed nor desired as the gift of tender, compassionate, forgiving love. And even this gift may fall very short of its intended powers, if in your giving, you do not make this love felt until it is an actual thing in the lives of your children. If they do not feel this love as an actual thing they will grow up lacking in their development. Yea, you must, by your sincere love, teach them also to love. As they return your love you will have done more for them than if you gave them half the world. Teach them to participate in giving love. Do not demand it of them. Love cannot be commanded. It has to be won. And giving love alone brings the great out-pouring glory of its divine power coursing through your being and on out to the world. As you give forth love from your opened heart it will return unto you multiplied and clothed in eternal power.

Paternal love has often been a one-sided offering, not a beautiful partnership. And the children have been cheated for they have not learned the joy and the power of returning or giving the divine gift of love. They have not learned to open their own precious hearts to the great out-flowing, inpouring power of life itself, nor comprehended the everlasting glory and joy of it.

When your children are brought up in this love there will be no more distraught, problem children, for the great healing can come. The healing will come first to those who send out the love, then to those who receive it. Then it can go out to help heal the nations for love is the fruit that will heal the bleeding, suffering world. With you, my dearly beloved, this great healing must start. From you it must begin to be shed forth. Get the fountain of your own heart opened and the seal removed, and all else will be added unto you.

Yea, it is more blessed to give than to receive, for as you give, the blessing is your own. The more you give the more you have and the greater will be your power of bestowing. Within the power to give the perfect love is also the power of perfect health, perfect beauty, perfect power, yea, even The "Fullness of the Father", and Life Eternal.

Chapter XV.

THE RAZOR'S EDGE

It has been said, and rightly so, that this road of enlightenment is "The Razor's Edge."

It is the fine edged blade that cuts off those who are not willing to make the full sacrifice of the little petty "self". It is the knife that cuts out the weaknesses and failings of those who determinedly cling to its sharpened edge. It is the pruning knife of the Father, who is the husbandman. It cuts away the excesses, the useless leaves, the dead and cluttering branches and twigs, that each living branch might be ever more alive, more perfect and stronger and productive in the bearing of the Fruit of the precious Tree of Life.

Know, beloved, that the season is at hand for this divine Tree of Life to begin to bear its precious fruit. And its fruit is Love! Its fruit is the love of God that is shed forth in the hearts of the children of men. And humanity is the branches, and I Am the Vine.

The pruning knife of the Father is truly the razor's edge. And for those who are not sincere the edge is dangerous. For those who are not a-flame with true desire this razor's edge is impossible to cross over. For those who love their faults and failings it is most difficult. For those who love God it is easy and a pathway of glory, though it is a straight and narrow way, and difficult to fulfill, for it is the "overcoming of the self". It is the pathway of Eternal Life. It is the path that leads to the very throne of God and fulfills the great Amen.

Yea, beloved, this razor's edge, this pruning knife of the Father will cut away your excess burdens of failures and weaknesses. As you grow it becomes more sharp and more keen until you become purified by its refining and its pruning. As you, in full consciousness become aware that you are one of the divine branches of the Tree of Life and permit Me to become the Living, life-giving Vine, all the excesses and weaknesses of your being will be pruned away and you will become perfect and glorious.

The words of Isaiah tell of it, describing it as the glorified road to Zion, the pure in heart, or the way of the purification of the heart. "And a highway shall be there, AND A WAY, and It shall be called the way of Holiness; The unclean shall not pass over it; but it shall be for those: The wayfaring man, though fools shall not err therein." And when the pure in heart come to Zion, "They shall come singing songs of everlasting joy." And their joy shall be the Fullness of the Father and in it shall be contained that great inner song of divine ecstasy and love and praise and rejoicing and thanksgiving that will overcome the darkness and negatives and evils. Yea, beloved, and you shall take My Name upon you, my great Unspeakable Name, and you shall be clothed in Light, the Light of my presence.

And the unclean shall not pass over the razor's edge, though fools shall not err therein. For the way is plain, and the path is straight. Yea, I Am the Way, the Truth and the Light.

It is true that few have stood the test of knowing God. And this test is the test of purification. But for you, beloved and anointed, the New Day is dawning and the way will be made easy and you shall have the power to fulfill, for the map to the Highway shall be placed in your hands. Only you must travel it. The journey is yours to make.

My sacred book "Ye Are Gods" revealed the vision to those who had eyes to see and the Holy Spirit of Promise bore witness to the worthy ones that it could be fulfilled in them. And now to fulfill my promise that I would give no commandment save I would prepare the way for its fulfillment, I have spoken these words to you, for you are mine and I know you. I ordained you for this work before ever you were born.

Yea, beloved, my holy anointed, step forth and claim your birthright, for the time is at hand. Be ye a bearer of the Tree of Life that its fruit of divine Love might be shed forth through you. Such is the Fruit that will heal the nations.

And Lo, I Am with you always, even unto the end. Amen and Amen.

Chapter XVI.

"THOUGH YOUR SINS BE AS SCARLET"

"Sin is the breaking of the law." It is the transgression against the laws of progress. Yea, beloved, the breaking of the laws is living contrary or out of tune with the great loving rules necessary for your own perfection and glory and happiness and abundance of all good.

Whether you live up to the laws given or not, makes no difference to the Father. They were not revealed out of eternity for Him, nor for His benefit. They were brought forth for you. Only you can be injured if you fail to fulfill such holy laws as have been revealed through the goodness and mercy of our Divine Father of love. God cannot be hurt nor injured by anything you do, or fail to do. You can only hurt yourself if you persist in wrongdoing. But know this, every law was given for your glory and profit and joy and progress. They are formed out of eternity and they are eternal and cannot be changed. The laws were given, not to restrict you, nor to make you miserable and unhappy, but as eternal principles upon which your soul must progress into its eternal glory of complete fulfillment.

There are eternal laws concerning all things eternal. Mathematics, chemistry, music, harmony and the perfection of yourself in mind, body and soul are all based upon eternal laws that cannot be put aside if the right solution is to be obtained. These eternal laws existed long before this world began. They will exist long after this world has fulfilled its destiny for they are eternal. These divine laws of our Almighty Father were not meant to be a stumbling block to you. They were given to bring about your own ultimate good, your own happiness and perfection and progress and complete joy. None of the laws of God are restricting in joy. The laws of God alone can bring a fullness of joy. They do not bring a wild hysteria. These laws fulfill the divine majesty of dignity and inward rejoicing that vibrates in turn with the glorified melody of the Universe. This is the great joy that is beyond expression, beyond anything which can can possibly express and when one tries to express it in shouting, or physical expression he is but profaning its majesty of dignified power of fulfillment. It is the power and majesty and dignity of all good. It is a joy of spirit which overcomes all doubts, fears, all *lightmindedness* and darkness and could never be expressed in unseemly shouting nor babblings nor undignified actions. Within this joy is contained the singing power of divine majesty and poise and purity.

It is the narrow little rituals and rules which men have formulated which are the restrictors of joy and bind my children down with long, sanctimonious faces. Such laws and creeds are formed by men who know not God. Take, for instance, beloved, the feeling you receive over any good act you do, any service you render, every precious smile given, every kind word spoken and realize that if you went out shouting about the good received it would be instantly dissipated. These small, momentary actions you do, bring to you but a taste of the great joy you will receive if you will but take upon you my yoke and begin to work toward the fulfilling of the whole law. Partake, oh beloved, of the power of obedience. Yea, bask in the unspeakable glory of forgiveness that you might be forgiven. Glory in the immeasurable joy of love, love so pure, so divine, so Christ-like and forgiving and merciful that it can go forth to heal and bless a world. Then you will comprehend the joy of which I speak, the joy that is spiritual and which is developed in a sober and controlled mind, a mind that has overcome all light-mindedness, frivolity and discordant, evil thinking.

Whenever the power and Spirit of God is expressing, there is joy. In the sunshine, in the flower, in the song of the bird, in the gurgling of the brook, in the growth of a tree, in the rhythm of the rain is the boundless vibration of singing joy and ecstasy being offered up to the throne of God.

In the laws of righteousness is contained your joy, for they are for you, not against you. These holy laws are for your own happiness and progress and growth and infinite, eternal joy and everlasting glory.

Because the laws of God, or progress, are eternal they cannot be put aside to admit any sin, nor make any sin right by giving it the sanction of the Father. It is impossible to change the laws of mathematics. It is impossible to change the laws of your progress for they are heavenly laws and are irrevocable and cannot be changed, not even by God, for He is unchangeable, otherwise He would cease to be God. And He ceaseth not to be God, and He changes not. Neither can His laws be changed to admit your transgressions.

It is because the laws are eternal that sin cannot be allowed, or "looked upon with the least degree of allowance". You have your free agency to serve sin if you choose, but then you are no longer free, but the servant of sin. Those who have made sin their master always blaspheme against God, giving Him the blame for the consequences. The way of the sinner is hard and brings naught but unhappiness, misery and despair. And sin is not allowed upon the pathway of perfection.

"Damnation" is the same whether it is spelled with an "n" or without it. When the stream or river is dammed the progress of the waters is stopped and it cannot go on. When my children are damned by the blocks or walls they have placed in their own paths their progress is stopped and they are damned. Their suffering is with them and of their own making, and will continue to increase. It will be intensified when they realize that they have been left far behind as they fed only upon the "evil" of the tree of knowledge. The "good" will be theirs only when they leave the evil behind or overcome it. Then will the "evil", with its consequent suffering, be used for "good". This is true if one has not remained too long in sin, or sinned too much to be forgiven in this world. *Or in the world to come,* which is possible. There is no possible progress as long as the sin remains. The joy, the victory, the progress and glory is for him who "overcomes".

Dearly beloved children of mine, you must understand that it is your own sins that block your progress and retard you, holding you back from all that is perfect and beautiful and good. Your own great destiny and divine pattern of fulfillment is unrealized because you have rejected the laws of their completion and bringing forth. Yea, beloved, you alone block your progress for it is impossible to go and to stay at the same time. If you fulfill or live the laws you have to progress.

You, who love your sins more than you love Me, and will therefore not let them go, must continue to carry them until the burden of them becomes so great your hearts will break under the unendurable load.

If in that hour of supreme anguish and despair, you turn unto Me and offer Me your broken hearts and give me your burdens, I will be able to help place your feet upon the pathway of Light.

If your sins are so great upon you that you are completely enslaved by them and have no strength within you with which to fight, then call upon My Name for help to overcome. And

I promise you that whenever you call upon Me for help to overcome some sin or weakness or unrighteous desire I will be there. As long as you call upon Me I shall never fail to give you help and comfort and strength.

And when you learn to love me more than you love your sin or weakness the unrighteousness will be cast from you as the throwing off of the shackling chains of bondage and you shall stand free. You must understand however, that you will continue to serve that which you love most, Me, or the sin. Only as you give me your love, and as you love God with all your heart, soul, mind and strength can you have the power to rise above the sin and completely overcome it.

If, at first, you lack the faith, the full desire, or the great love, then call upon My Name and I will give you of my strength.

Yea, I invite you now to come and place your hand in mine that you be not left behind as the race of men move on upward into the Light. You must realize that even your slightest sin will detain you and keep you from fulfilling all that has been promised unto you.

And now, my beloved, I would give again the sacred keys on which the forgiveness of your sins is based: "Forgive and you shall be forgiven."

Those who cannot forgive cannot be forgiven. The very power of being forgiven is contained in the ability to forgive. Those who carry their grudges and hates and spirit of retaliation with them are carrying a burden of such deep darkness they become actually clothed in the darkness of their own dislikes. And so I speak gently these words, for all have sinned; your own great release will come when you can forgive. If you cannot forgive you are carrying upon your shoulders your neighbor's, or brother's, failures and transgressions and you are also carrying the burden of your own sins, weaknesses, innumerable errors and mistakes.

When I commanded you to judge not, lest you be judged I was revealing the great eternal law by which you could escape the great judgment.

Surely the burden of your own mistakes is enough to bear. Why carry your neighbor's also?

Know, my children, that your weaknesses are realities of bondage and damnation, for your progress is stopped by them. No matter how trivial your sins, your faults and failings may appear to you, for you are prone to excuse your individual mistakes and weaknesses, they are your stumbling blocks. And it is impossible for God to look upon sin with the least degree of allowance, for in God's rules sin cannot be allowed. He may have compassion on the sinner, but for the sin there is no allowance whatsoever. The sin and the weakness has to be left behind before you can go on.

Whatever your sins and weaknesses are you may be sure that you have, or had at least five of them, not counting the seal of a hardened heart and a blinded mind, which have, or should have been removed before this record came into your hands. Most of my children carry the burden of an unforgiving heart, and therefore they are weighted down with both their neighbor's and their own weaknesses and transgressions.

Yea, it is true that "I give men weaknesses that they might become strong". For in the "overcoming" does your strength lie and your power increase.

Know this, beloved children of mine, that something cannot be made out of nothing. But out of darkness, out of fear and failure and negation can be brought forth conditions that are positive if you will use them aright. Yea, error can be transmuted into strength. The very energy contained in the negative condition can be trasmuted into dynamic, potent, living power. Transmuted energy always serves as a leverage to lift you higher. Yea, years of striving can be accomplished in one great stride by using the power of ill as a leverage to transform the condition. All the power of the negatives, the hates and dislikes and fears still exist, but they are "converted" into good by overcoming them. The power and energy of these transformed forces are immeasurable and they are yours to use, for they will become subjected unto you and will be transformed into forces of Life and Light as you OVERCOME.

The power contained in any condition of negativism and darkness and transgression can be tremendous when overcome by the power of love and a desire to serve God. And always their power is yours to use, my beloved, if you will reach out your hand and bring them under control. Use your failures to obtain wisdom, your weaknesses to become strong, your sins to learn the power of forgiving compassion and your suffering to perfect the gift of obedience. In this way the whole law can be fulfilled in you. And you can be prepared to receive "The Fullness of the Father" by your own purification. All that is necessary in this great transition, my beloved, is for you to change your way of thinking and your way of feeling. Yea, gather to you the gift of divine compassion and mercy and you shall receive mercy. Forgive and you shall be forgiven. Love and the gates of eternity will begin to open and you will become a divine bearer of the very Fruit of the Tree of Life. Yea, all things will become subjected unto you and you will be filled with glory and with Light. This is your true dominion. Yea, power is yours to subdue the earth and all conditions upon it.

Suffering, which is caused by your own attitudes and thoughts, is to teach you obedience. And the full and complete obedience to the will of God contains the pattern of your own perfection, the complete fulfillment of all glory, in you. In the gift of divine obedience is contained the glory of your own majesty, the fullness of your joy and all that is possible for you to receive from the loving abundance of your Father.

Within the gift of obedience is the power to completely overcome the "self". When you desire God's will more than you desire anything else, when you can enjoy your misery, or any heartbreak or calamity, not in self-pity, but in gratitude to accept the will of God, the evil will begin to flee from you. Even the evil of your own creating will be dissolved. And there will be no more suffering. Within this law of gratitude is also contained the promise: "He who is thankful in all things shall be made glorious, and the things of this earth shall be added unto him an hundred-fold; yea, more."

And now, lest you hold to your sins and wallow in them, or permit them to hold you bound let me speak these loving words of beautiful mercy and compassion; "that you stand not forever in your sins": "Though their sins be as scarlet, they shall be white as snow, TO HIM THAT OVERCOMETH." Beautiful, beloved children, none are without sin. He who says he is without sin is a liar and the truth is not in him. The great glory is in the power of "overcoming."

Sometimes the greatest sin is the blindness which blinds ones eyes, that he sees not his own sins, failings and transgressions, but only his neighbors.

And now, I call aloud unto the ends of the earth, that you need no longer remain in your sins. Yea, it is time again for the Tree of Life to bear its precious Fruit of healing and Eternal Life. Come beloved, that you might be prepared to not only partake of the great feast of the Lord, but be a bearer of the Fruits which will be served at the feast. Yea, come unto me, and I will give you the bread and waters of life freely.

Yea, come! And though your sins be as scarlet

they shall be white as snow, TO HIM WHO OVERCOMETH.

Yea, look up and comprehend the power of my promises unto you. Acknowledge your sins and weaknesses to yourselves, then bring them unto me, for I am your confessor, and your sins concern naught but yourselves, those whom you have injured or wronged by your transgressions and Me. Yea, bring them to me, and go thy way and sin no more.

Gather up your prides, your prejudices, your hates, your fears and jealousies and lusts and selfishness and bring them to me for surely you have been heavy laden. Yea, come, and I will give you rest. Come, and I will gather you under my wing! Be not afraid, it is I. It is true that I do not look upon sin with the least degree of allowance, but for you who will bring your burden of sin to me, I will give you of my strength that you might overcome.

Justice is for those who do not overcome, who continue to enjoy their sins and transgressions and who seek to justify and condone them. For such is justice ordained. But mercy is for those who come unto me and ask for power to overcome. For such is mercy given. Develop mercy within you and you shall obtain mercy, even as forgiveness is for those who forgive. In the power of forgiving is contained the pure, divine, Christ-like compassion that brings its healing mercy and reveals the power to overcome.

Yea, come unto me, and though your sins be as scarlet, they will become white as snow, TO YOU WHO OVERCOME. The overcoming must be accomplished within you. It is in your hands. And the greatest overcoming is to eliminate every desire for sin. This is the plan and the path whereby you may rise above your weaknesses, your trials and temptations, if you so desire, and enter again into my presence.

To you who receive these teachings, in which a fool may not err, and abide them not, your condemnation will be greater. "To whom much is given, much is required."

Beloved, I have never given a commandment save I prepared the way for its fulfillment. Know that no promise nor word of mine was ever given in vain, nor will they return unto me void and unfulfilled, they will all be fulfilled.

When the command was given for you to "Be perfect even as your Father in Heaven is perfect", it was definite and possible else it would not have been given. And that command still stands. It has not been revoked. Down the centuries it has stood as an open challenge, waiting for you who could begin to believe in my words and in my teachings. Yea, it has stood waiting for you, my beloved, who will endeavor to live by my words that you might learn of the power contained in them. And that you might KNOW whether they are of God, or not. Yea, these greatest of all teachings have waited for you who have the faith to believe, and the desire to live by them and to fulfill the holy promises and learn of the power of Godliness.

Only in this day have there been those who are great enough to believe and to begin to fulfill, though these words have stood open and calling down the centuries. They are timeless and eternal. Neither can they fail, for those who will take hold of them. Yea, "All things are possible to you who believe."

To you who die in your sins, and that is how all die, for you truly die because of your own sins and not for Adam's transgressions, know that for you is awaiting the Judgment. And in that Judgment will be revealed every transgression, every flaw, every weakness, every mistake, even your secret acts and thoughts. For you who pass through this Judgment there will be only justice.

But for you, beloved, who overcome, there is no Judgment. For as you overcome your sins will be blotted out, even that they will never come in remembrance before the Lord. This is mercy! And this is my gift to you! For this I gave my Life! I did not give my life that you could continue in your sins and escape the consequences and obtain mercy and be held unaccountable for your transgressions. I gave my life that you might comprehend the pattern by which you too might overcome, that by believing in my promises and laying hold of my word you could follow the pattern I gave, that you too might overcome, even as I overcame.

If you have faith and a desire to fulfill my words then come and take my hand and I will help you to fulfill all things, yea, all the great and mighty promises made unto the children of men.

Yea, how could you be born of the Spirit unless that Spirit, which is given to abide in you, begins to direct you to God, and to open your understandings that you might comprehend the power of "Godliness", and become Godly?

And after you are born of the Spirit how can you reach the full maturity, even the "Fullness of the Father", which has been promised from the beginning, save you continue to hunger and thirst after righteousness? Is not the main desire of an infant born of the flesh, a desire and crying for food, that its body might grow? And so it is for those who are born of the Spirit.

There must needs be the continual hungering and thirsting after righteousness. There must be a constant desiring for more and more of my great truths, which is the Spiritual food by which the Spirit must grow. Yea, it is only the continual hungering after spiritual food that can fulfill and complete your divine maturity, even until you receive of the "Fullness of the Father".

All sins and weaknesses, no matter what they are, are easy to overcome when you desire to serve me more than you desire to transgress.

And when you serve me, as you think, you are only serving yourselves and bringing to pass all perfection and all glory for yourselves. In the complete fulfilling of the two first and Great Commandments is the power to overcome all sin, cast out all fear, fulfill all perfection. Live them and see if they do not contain the very power to comprehend and know God, and Me, whom He sent, that you might receive Life Eternal.

Yea, "And the Spirit and the bride say, Come. And let him that heareth say, Come. And let him that is athirst come. And whosoever will, let him take of the water of life freely," that he reach his maturity and receive of my fullness and be purified, even as I am pure. FOR THE DAY IS AT HAND.

Chapter XVII.

"I CAME TO FULFILL THE LAW"

Dearly beloved, let not this work disturb you, nor think that it has come to destroy the law. "I came not to destroy the law, but to fulfill it." These higher laws came not to destroy the truths you have, but to fulfill them that you might pass beyond the symbols they contain, on to the complete fulfillment of all symbols and laws into the great reality of All-Truth. These higher laws I gave, and am again verifying for everyone who seeks to know my Name, and the power thereof, even my great Unspeakable Name. This is the Name which you are commanded to take upon you and then it becomes yours to bear when you begin to fulfill *all* the laws and the prophets, or every promise ever given by me, or by My Father, or any of the Holy Prophets since the beginning of time.

Know, beloved, that "He who asketh in the Spirit, asketh according to the will of God. And he shall receive even as he asketh." When you ask in the Spirit it is necessary that you enter into that great inner vibration of joy and thanksgiving and gratitude and inward glory. As you enter into this great Light you will truly ask according to the Will of God, for no selfish, petty desires abide in that Light and everything you ask for will be according to the Will of God. And it will be granted unto you, for such is the promise. It is in this vibration of love and gratitude and holiness that you take upon you MY NAME, and anything you ask "in" that Name, or vibration of Spirit, shall be granted unto you. Yea, take upon you this holy vibration of praise and love and gratitude and you shall know that I abide in you and you abide in me. Come into this vibration of inner ecstasy of pure joy and grateful thanksgiving and you will know the power of my words and receive the fulfillment of them: "How often would I have gathered you, even as a hen gathers her chickens under her wings, and ye would not."

Now is the time, my beloved, when you must hear my voice and come into this vibration of inner glory and abide in the strength of my power, and take upon you My Name, for now is the time for all laws to be fulfilled and the great Truth be revealed that you might be free. Yea, "Know the Truth, and the Truth shall make you free; and he who is free shall be free indeed." Yea, you will no longer be under the law for the law will have been fulfilled in you.

When you have cast out all ugliness of soul, bitterness of thought, your malice, jealousy, hates and discords you will have overcome the darkness and will have the power to pass on into the great love and Light and receive of my atonement, or "at-one-ment" and will truly become one with me. Even as I Am one with my Father. I placed this petition at the throne of my Father centuries ago, in your behalf. And now is the time of its fulfillment, for my prayers were not in vain, neither can my word return unto me void and unfulfilled.

You, beloved, must hear my voice, then open the door of your heart, yea, even the door of your soul, and "Lo I will come in and feast with you, and you with me." And our feasting will be upon the bread of life, even the very Fruit of the Tree of Life, or the great love. Then shall you also partake of the waters of life freely. And nothing again shall ever touch your lives to hurt you or make you afraid. And all mourning and all crying shall cease and you shall receive even a fullness of my joy. And you shall abide in me forever, for I know you and you are mine, even my elect.

Yea, beloved, you who hear my voice and know me, know my voice is love. And in love

I now speak to you to prepare you for the great day that is at hand.

First my voice was unto those of Israel and they rejected me. Now my voice is unto all, even unto the end of the earth. "And the first shall be last; and the last shall be first." Yea, along the highways and the byways of the earth my voice is calling to you. Yea, to the halt and the lame and the blind, and to the meek and the humble, to the mighty and the strong, to the least and to the great. Open your souls to hear, and come, follow me! Yea, fulfill the laws which I fulfilled. And by this great Light of Christ, which is given to abide in you, you shall have power to overcome all things, even the "self".

In this pathway, or highway, that leads to the purifying of the heart, even to Zion, every desire for sin must be left behind, every lustful, sensual craving, every petty desire for sin, every shred of darkness, and especially must you overcome your desires to be exalted above your brothers. You must give up every ambition for credit and reward and with your eyes single to the glory of God, follow the highway of Light, even the highway of purification, which shall reveal Him to you and you shall behold His face. This is the highway which the wicked cannot travel, but in which a fool cannot err. Yea,

I Am the Way, the way of purification, within.

Yea, purify your hearts with your songs of everlasting joy! Yea, "come singing to Zion", the "pure in heart." Yea, prepare yourselves for the great feast, even the feast of the Lamb.

Pray always and doubt not! Yea, fear not, for lo, I am with you always! And by the Light of my power shall all things be fulfilled in you. Yea, nothing is impossible to him who believes. Only the unbelievers have no part in me, nor in the glory which is mine.

In my great love for you I shall repeat my words which I gave unto my servant Malachi and I desire to inform you that they shall truly be fulfilled in you who believe in me:

"Then they that feared the Lord spake often one to another; and the Lord hearkened, and heard it, and a book of remembrance was written before him for them that loved the Lord, *and that thought upon His Name.*

"And they shall be mine, saith the Lord of hosts, in that day when I make up my jewels; and I will spare them as a man spareth his own son that serveth him.

"Then shall ye return, and discern between the righteous and the wicked, between him that serveth God and him that serveth him not."

These are my words unto you, my beloved,

in this day. And let no one take from you the right to speak often one to another upon the power of My Name, nor let them take from you the power to turn unto me in every thought Yea, gather in your homes with your friends and loved ones and talk upon these holy things and pray unto me, and I will hear.

Many are commanding that you give them your thoughts, forbidding such gatherings of prayer and to speak upon my Holy Name, and they are not of me. See that you do not let them freeze your minds and enslave your souls that you be left desolate for having trusted in the arm of flesh. "Cursed is he who trusteth in the arm of flesh", for he has failed to come to Me, and receive of my Light and be guided by My Voice, and to progress along my Holy Highway of purification.

I admonish you, my dearly beloved, to turn unto me in every thought, doubt not the power of God. Doubt not that He can hear your prayers and will answer them, especially when you ask for wisdom to know Truth. Let none take from you the right to come to me direct, lest you be seized with the chains of hell and find no escape. Know that he who asks and he who seeks and he who knocks is obeying the command of God. Therefore I command that you let none tell you that God cannot hear and answer your prayers, for by so doing they are denying the very power of God. Know that your prayers are heard, and that they do not ascend unto me in vain.

Neither let any tell you that the power of the Holy Ghost cannot lead *you* into all truth, for by so doing they are denying the power of the Holy Ghost, and woe be unto them! Those who are teaching that you cannot be taught of me and that I will not hear and answer your prayers are teaching contrary to the law and order of God. And as they teach that they alone have the power to bestow the gift of the Holy Ghost, yet by their teachings they deny that you have the power to receive it, making their own ministry in vain. Know that the gift and power of the Holy Ghost is to lead you into all truth. Know that God is no respecter of persons. Know that he that cometh to God shall be acknowledged. Know that the power of the Holy Ghost will lead you into all truth, even until you comprehend all truth, and those who deny this power are denying the power of God and the Gift of the Holy Ghost and woe be unto them!

Yea, beloved, now is the time when all my holy laws and my holy promises must begin to be fulfilled in you. Just where you are, from the streets and the alleys and the tenements and the mansions, from the cities and the farms, I invite you to come. And my sheep hear my voice, and they know me.

Yea, come! All ye ends of the earth, for my voice is Spirit, and my Spirit is Truth. So be it, AMEN.

CHAPTER XVIII.

THE WAY OF TRANSGRESSION IS HARD

My BELOVED, when anything is written by the finger of God you are to understand henceforth what is meant, for all things are to be made known unto you, for you are to be as wise as serpents, and as harmless as doves. A finger, outstretched, is a pointer of the way. It reveals the path and indicates clearly and distinctly the road one must travel to return into my presence and the presence of My Father.

The book "Ye Are Gods" was written wholly by the finger of God and included in it are all districts. It was promised to the world centuries ago, by my servant, the writer of the Odes of Solomon, my dearly beloved, even my faithful one. Its coming forth was foretold, for "surely I will do nothing except I will reveal it to my servants, the prophets." You who have had the faith and the purity of heart to comprehend the vision contained in this sacred record and who have tried to follow the path it outlines shall have the needed help required to fulfill it. To you who hold to the pathway mapped by the finger of God shall be given the strength and help required to return unto me to behold my face if you will but continue, and doubt not. For you was it given, and for you was it sent forth. In it is contained the fulfilling of my holy promise to the world.

He who says he is of me and heeds not my words, nor follows the path I have indicated has nothing to do with me, and is not mine.

Behold! I am Jesus Christ, the first and last, and if you abide in my laws, then are you mine. Then it is that you have claim upon my promises, for if you do as I say, then am I bound.

Know you not that no man was ever damned for believing too much? Man is only damned for believing too little.

If you had studied my word with a contrite spirit you would have comprehended the continual stress placed upon the transgression of UN-BELIEF, and you would know that it is the unbelievers who are damned. Yea, you would realize that the great wickedness of unbelief has sealed up the blessings of heaven, even those great and unspeakable blessings that have been hid up from the foundation of the world, because of unbelief. This is the great unbelief that has been caused because of the hardness of men's hearts and the blindness of their minds. Yea, you would have read my words in Titus: 1:15: "Unto them that is unbelieving, is nothing pure." And it is so. "And they call that which is good evil, and they deny the power of God, and the gift of the Holy Ghost, and woe be unto them."

Know you not that unbelief renders fruitless and ineffectual?

Yea, search my words that are written upon the ancient records, if you cannot hear my Living Voice and come to me direct, and learn of the condemnation that is created within yourself because of unbelief. For know you not that any creed and doctrine that seals your minds against more light and more truth is accounted as evil, for it will damn you and stop your progress?

The sin of unbelief is the greatest of all sins. All the carnal transgressions that can be committed are against your own lives, your fellowmen and against the world. But the sin of unbelief is against your own soul and against God, the Father. If this sin is great enough it is also against the Holy Ghost, and such sin cannot be forgiven in this world, nor in the world to come.

It is impossible for a child of God to believe too much, for as your faith is, so shall it be unto you, if your hearts are pure before me. Such deep belief must always be pure, unaspiring,

[171]

humble and divine, with eyes wholly single to the glory of God. Yea, beloved, the command for you to "believe" does not mean for you to believe in fulfilling your personal lusts, or your own evil desires, such as the lust for many women, or high and mighty honors, above your fellow men, or any of the carnal yearnings of the flesh. It means to believe in the promise of God, those divine promises of purity and holiness and fulfillment.

Yea, let the same mind which was also in Christ, Jesus, who thought it not robbery to be equal with God."

Lift up your eyes, my beloved, "for the land thou seest will I give unto thee." If you can truly lift up your eyes unto me you shall behold the great and marvelous things which I have laid up for you, from the foundation of the world, and which has not come unto you because of UNBELIEF. All promises are yours, and they will be fulfilled unto you, if you are not numbered among the unbelievers.

And again, I say, "No man was ever damned for believing too much, but for believing too little, if his belief is pure and undefiled, with eyes single to the glory of God.

If you believe in the negative things of life, then they are yours too. If you see naught but

evil, believe naught but evil, then you will become the evil which you behold. If you hold to
sin, believing in its power over you, then you become the sin which you behold. And God cannot look upon sin with the least degree of allowance. Only your sins have separated you from
me, and the greatest of all sins is UNBELIEF.

God may have compassion for the sinner, but
as long as the sin is accepted and remains there
is no hope for an approach to my throne. And
for him who lingers too long in his sins, his way
becomes hedged up and he will find, too late,
that he has become the sin he has nourished in
his heart. Then he has become secured by the awful chains of darkness, which he, himself has
welded in his own lusts, his own transgressions,
and evil.

Nay, there is no excuse, nor allowance for sin
or unbelief. They are not of God but are of your
own choosing.

My promises belong to those who "overcome". Yea, beloved, you must overcome even
"every desire for sin". You, my dearly beloved,
are the gold that must be tried in the fire. You
must be purified in the furnace that the dross
and imperfections might be consumed and purged out and purified, or cast away. As you follow me you must also overcome, even as I over-

came. These are the works that I did, which you also must do. It is required of you who would behold my face, to overcome the laws of the flesh, even as I overcame the weaknesses of the flesh and subdued all things under my feet.

Yea, you also must overcome, even as I overcame, for these are my words, and my works, which ye must fulfill. "To him that overcometh will I grant to sit down with me in my throne, even as I overcame and am sat down with my Father in his throne."

And, according to my words unto my servant, John, were these sayings given to you that you might ponder and fulfill: "To him that overcometh will I grant to eat of the Tree of Life, which is in the midst of the Paradise of God."

"Yea, he that overcometh shall not be hurt of the second death.

"To him that overcometh will I give to eat of the hidden manna, and will give him a white stone, and in the stone a new name written, which no man knoweth saving he that receiveth it.

"Yea, he that overcometh, and keepeth (or doeth) my WORKS unto the end (of his testing), to him I give power over the nations; and he shall rule them with a rod of iron (which is my word); as the vessels of a potter shall they be broken to shivers; even as I received of my Father. And I will give him the morning star.

"He that overcometh, the same shall be clothed in white raiment (that the shame of his nakedness will never appear); and I will not blot his name out of the Book of Life, but I will confess his name before my Father, and before his angels, and such will be heralded throughout the realms of my Father's Kingdom."

But, my beloved, the way of overcoming is yours to travel. No one can overcome for you. You must believe and step forth into the way, which may seem impossible, and there you will find me. All promises await you if you will but believe in my words and desire to fulfill them, more than you desire to continue in your sins. You must commence the work of accomplishment. Then when you have done everything possible and your strength fails mine will begin, if you will but ask, seek and knock. For nothing is impossible to him who believes.

If you are bound by sin and believe in the sin, more than you believe in me, then you are bound indeed. If you desire your sin more than you desire me, then no help can reach you, for you have rejected it and cast it aside for the love you have for your vices.

When you desire me more than you desire your sins, your lusts and your vices, then it is easy to overcome, with my help. As long as you desire, and seek and ask I will never forsake you. It is no sin to be weak, but it is weak to sin. And in either case my strength and power is but awaiting your outstretched hand to give you aid. I never forsake those who call upon my Name.

Believe in me and in my holy promises and the bands of sin can be broken. And though your transgressions are as scarlet, to you who overcometh, they shall be white as snow, for you shall be purified.

CHAPTER XIX.

THE WILL OF GOD

To you, my most dearly beloved, who have felt the touch of my hand upon you as you have read this work, and who have felt my love enfold you and my Spirit yearning over you, I now speak.

The gold that is tried in the fire, which you are instructed to buy of me, is the pure gold of your own soul.

The gold, or soul that is completely refined for use must be purged in the furnace, for I Am the purifier of pure gold, and I "sit with my fan in my hand."

In olden times, when I trod upon the shores of Gallilee and lingered with men, in my sojourn upon earth, gold was refined by intense burning. The dross rose to the top and was drained away. The gold was then placed in new cauldrons, and the purifying continued as occasionally the refiner leaned over the cauldron to gaze into the molten ore. When it was completely purified the refiner would behold his own face reflected in its golden depths as the vapors would separate as he waved his fan. Yea, I am the purifier of gold and I sit with my fan in my hand. And when you are purified for use my face will be reflected in you, my thoughts made apparent in you, my love made manifest through you.

Yea, "You must be tested and tried in all things," even until the dross is cast away and the evils purified and transmuted into good. Then as the molten cauldron reflects my face so will my face be reflected in you and you shall see me and know that I Am. Yea, beloved, when your heart is pure you will behold my face. This is my eternal promise unto all men.

Yea, come to Zion, the place, or state, of the complete purification of your heart. And you will behold me there.

And now, the last step of the journey to Zion must be revealed unto you, for it is my finger that is writing this record. It is my finger that is pointing the way back into my presence.

Come! Follow me!

If your sufferings have been great, if your purging has been intense, and at times, seemingly unbearable, then lift up your head and rejoice. For know this, my beloved, suffering is only given to teach obedience, or to purge out the wilfullness within your own heart, to help you overcome the desire for transgression.

When you have learned obedience by the things you have suffered then there is no more need for suffering. Yea, when you can love the suffering, for my sake, then will the suffering flee from you. Then indeed, will you be able to rejoice in your tribulation and thank God for every trial and every heartbreak and all your troubles. You will understand fully, when you reach the point of such divine purification, the glory of the things I now speak to you. You will comprehend that the suffering is but the fires of the furnace of purification. Then will you be able to commune with me face to face and know that my promises fail not.

You must also understand that the burning does not turn the dross into gold. If you desire to be evil, if you hold to your sins and glory in your wickedness, then are you the dross and have become the sin. And after the burning you are cast out upon the refuse heap, defiled, worthless, unglorified and unredeemed. Even the pure gold of your own hearts will be extracted from you and you will be left unto yourself and be consumed by the second death, which eliminates the dross and dregs of the rubbish heaps.

[179]

The choice is always yours, that is, up to a certain point. That point is a degree of transgression which completes the defilement of yourself and commits you to the dross, to be damned and rejected.

If your suffering has not helped to purify you, to refine you, to turn you to me, then it is because you have hardened your heart and have rebelled against my chastening rod, my pruning knife, or my refining fire. But understand this, the gold cannot be completely purified and refined without the heat of the furnace. The branch cannot bear perfect fruit without the pruner's knife. If you have grown hard and bitter under the divine tutorage of the Master, then have all your lessons been in vain and there is no more place for you in My Father's school, for whomsoever the Lord loveth he chasteneth. Yea, the Father is the husbandman, and the dead and lifeless, unproductive twigs (or traits) upon the branches must be trimmed away that you can stand forth in the strength of My glory, to bring forth much Fruit, the gift of love.

The remainder of my words are to you, beloved, who have not rebelled against the chastening hand of God, you who have learned obedience by the things you have suffered, for you are mine, and I know you.

To you, most dearly beloved, I now speak.

"Obedience is better than sacrifice." Not the obedience men would demand of you, for such obedience will damn your souls, for by it you become enslaved to the arm of flesh. The obedience of which I speak, is that loving, glorified obedience that makes you one with the divine Will of God. This is the obedience that completely overcomes the "self", the obedience that rejoices always, knowing naught and caring naught but for the will of God.

Yea, beloved, in that glorious obedience you become a vessel of purity in the hands of the Almighty Father. You become the fountain through which His perfect love pours forth to give life to a world.

In this obedience you take your place as a living branch and a bearer of the Fruit of the Tree of Life. This divine fruit is the pure love of God which must be shed forth through your heart. Yea, you shall be a bearer of the Fruit, which is God's pure love, the only Fruit containing the power of your own healing and the healing of the nations. Such is your divine destiny and for such were you brought forth.

Even as you are tested and tried in all things, and as the Father finds you are determined to serve Him at *ALL HAZARDS*, even to the loss of your families, your friends, your positions, your good names, your lives, and your souls, if necessary, then I seal upon you my holy promise that your sacred and holy calling and election is made sure, for you are mine.

And now, that you might know the last step in overcoming, that you may be truly followers of me, I say unto you that your wills must be yielded to the will of God, our Father.

When you can completely blend your will with Him, so that you desire only His Will, naught but His Will, though it be the cross, then indeed, will you be prepared to partake of my feast, even the feast of the Passover. Yea, for then you will be prepared to pass over from mortality into a higher phase of existence.

This giving of your will is not a letting go of effort, or feelings, or a stupid indifference of dead numbness. This giving of your will, completely to God, is the point of power, alive and vibrant with glory, though the cross awaits. It is the point of divine majesty. It is the complete surrender of the little mortal self, with all its desires, its personality, its petty yearnings, even to the giving up and complete surrender of all that you possess, your loved ones, when and if they turn against you, or if God requires them.

Yea, it is the supreme sacrifice of the broken heart.

Yea, as you relinquish your broken heart freely to Him, the surrender becomes a privilege and not a burden because of your love for His will. Then are you purified. Then you will find me, and my arms will be opened to you.

Know this, beloved, there is no glory in the heartbreak, nor is there any glory in the furnace of tribulation. The glory is produced as the gold is purified and yields its dross obtaining its eternal status of beauty and perfection. The process of refining holds naught of beauty. The glory is accomplished by your reaction to those things that take place in your life. The broken heart, when it is yielded up, and surrendered to God, is the offering supreme, the sacrifice divine. As you let go of your self-pity, your suffering and anguish and tears and personal will, relinquishing all to God, the great song of unspeakable glory will fill your soul and you will take upon you my Name, even the New Name which no tongue can utter. And you shall abide in that Name and its power will enfold you and you shall be clothed in Light, or the raiment of white.

Yea, beloved, accept thy cross! Rejoice in it, whatever it is! Embrace thy cross and glorify

the Name of God in songs of everlasting praise!
Let the worst befall thee that is possible to befall thee, if it is not of thy own doing, and rejoice in it, as though it were the Divine Will
of God. Sing forth thy songs of eternal thanksgiving from deep within thy heart, praise His
Holy Name and sorrow shall flee from thee, and
pain depart from thy life; and all sorrow and
tears will end, for you will have overcome them
as you step forth to fill a greater destiny in the
higher realms of Light.

I am telling this to you in "words" for this
is the language which you speak. But it can
never be fulfilled in words, for the fulfilling of
it is beyond all words. It can only be fulfilled
out of the very fibres of your heart and through
the strength of your soul.

As you surrender yourself to the Will of God
you will learn the perfection and glory of His
Will. In His Will is contained naught but beauty
and love and glory and perfection, your own
perfection, your own joy, your own complete
and eternal happiness, now, and forevermore.

Only your own fulfilling of this divine law can
reveal to you its unutterable glory. You will
realize fully that as you relinquish your will, my
most dearly beloved, that you do not become in-
sipid, or an inactive being. Nay, then is when

you truly become dynamic, powerful, stupendous, bearer of eternal Light.

Yea, as you relinquish your will, your own personal desires, aims, lusts, weaknesses, ambitions, or loved ones, you are also relinquishing your little, mortal self. It is crucified upon the altar or cross of obedience and utter surrender. Thus are the weaknesses lost and left behind. As you lose your life so shall you find it, yea even your greater life of power and fulfillment. Thus you become one with the power and majesty of the Almighty and receive even of His Fullness. Yea, then are you given power to "sit with me in my throne, even as I overcame and am sat down with my Father in His throne."

That, my beloved, is how you become the least, that you might become the servant of all; and how you truly become the greatest and have all things subjected unto you, both in heaven and on earth, the Life and the Light, the Spirit and the Power, sent forth by the Father, through Me, Jesus Christ, His Son. And so shall you become the sons of God and co-heirs with me.

Behold, my beloved, I stand with open arms, waiting to receive you.

Yea, most dearly beloved, you are a fountain through which the Living Waters must flow.

[185]

Yea, you are a branch that must be a bearer of the Fruit of the Tree of Life; yea, a bearer of my pure and eternal, healing, restoring, life-giving gift of love. This love must be shed forth through your heart to bring its healing to you, to your surroundings and to the nations. Yea, beloved, for you are mine.

When you learn to cast away the darkness, and to overcome it so that no thought or vibration is out of harmony with my divine love, then you will know the meaning of the promise, "Ye shall receive a fullness of joy!" Then shall you know also that "Joy is of the Saints, and none can put it on but they alone."

"And God shall wipe away all tears from your eyes, and there shall be no more death, neither sorrow, nor crying, neither shall there be any more pain; for these former things are past away.

"For behold, I make all things new.

"Yea, I am Alpha and Omega, the Beginning and the End. I will give unto him that is athirst of the fountain of the waters of life freely. And he that overcometh shall inherit all things; and I will be his God, and he shall be my son.

"But the *FEARFUL,* and the *UNBELIEV-ING,* and the abominable, and murderers, and whoremongers, and sorcerers, and idolaters, and all liars, shall have their part in the lake which burneth with remorse and eternal regret, which is the second death." For so I commanded my servant John to write. And My words are true and faithful, and they fail not.

CHAPTER XX.

YOUR ANOINTING OF LIGHT

Ten virgins will come forth to meet me and five of them will have oil in their lamps and five of them will not. And those who have the empty lamps will beseech those with oil to share their supply. And they will not, for they cannot.

The oil is my Spirit within, and none can give *It* to another. Neither can one syphon it from his associated no matter how much oil they have, or how brilliant their light is. That holy oil is my Spirit as it is permitted to flow through to bless and give one the power to let his light shine. And it must come forth from within.

This holy oil is supplied according to the need, even as in the case of the widow and her sons. It can flow forever as you require it to shed forth the light burning in your own hearts. It is always supplied according to your needs if you will but open up your hearts and souls, through love and gratitude, to permit it to circulate and come forth in its life-giving power.

This light, which you are commanded to let

shine forth, IS your anointing of light. Oil is the anointing fluid of God. Receive the oil of my Spirit and you shall be crowned with light, according to your degree of intelligence or awareness to use it.

When all light is withdrawn naught but darkness remains. Darkness is a lack of light. Withdraw the light, or let it go out, even temporarily through negative thinking, and you will be in darkness, darkness of mind and body and soul.

Withdraw all heat and only the cold remains.

To you, dearly beloved, is given the power to comprehend all things that you might know that the choice belongs to no other but yourselves.

"Despair cometh because of iniquity." It comes because you have not kept your awareness of the Light, or of the Spirit, and have permitted the flow of oil to cease. It is within your power to fill your lamps and to keep them burning, for the time is at hand, "for behold, the Bridegroom cometh."

As you hold your awareness of my power so shall you have my oil ever flowing forth in its holy, anointing power within you. This "awareness" is what is meant by the admonition "To turn to me in every thought." As you learn to hold your conscious awareness upon my Holy

[189]

Spirit you shall be anointed with the flame of the Spirit of Almighty God, our Father.

Whenever you permit fears or darkness to assail you, you must comprehend that it is because you are permitting your light to die down. You are shutting off the flow of that holy oil of my Spirit and you must, in that instant of realization, turn to me in complete love and trust, for only I can renew it.

Love, with its singing gratitude and thanksgiving, will keep the oil flowing until you actually become the Light.

To keep that holy oil flowing is the work which you must do. It is the work which I did. Whatsoever I did you can, and must, do also. Even greater works than I did, can you do.

The first work to be accomplished by you is the redemption of yourselves from your own darkness, from your fears and errors and mistakes and all negatives. Your first work is to prepare yourselves to be bearers of the Light of my Spirit by a complete purification of yourselves. It is accomplished by overcoming the darkness within you. When the darkness has been overcome then you may be sure that the Light within will begin to shine forth so that others, seeing your good works, will also begin

to glorify God by bringing forth that divine
Light within themselves.

It is not by words that one most glorifies
God. It is by becoming vessels of Light, through
which His Spirit might flow out in loving compassion to bless and heal a world of its hates
and fears and its darkness. This is the great
healing that is required. These are the greater
works of which I spoke. The individual, physical healings are not the greater works. The
greater works is to let your light so shine that
others may so desire that light within themselves
that they will open up their hearts to the pure
inflow of my anointing oil and the flame of
the Spirit of God, our Father. Then will their
own healing come. Thus all will be healed, and
all will have the power to do the works which
I did.

Your calling and election is not made sure
until you have made that divine Light of Christ
a permanent factor in your lives. Then you will
have overcome the jealousies, the fears, the darkness and all negatives. When all these have been
overcome by you, by becoming vessels of Light,
then will the last enemy fall. And death is the
last enemy to be overcome in your lives. And
it is you who must overcome it.

[191]

TO GOD THE GLORY

Come, my beloved, and do the works which I did, and know that my yoke is easy and my burden is Light. Yea, take upon you My Name, for My Name is power, even the power of eternal Light.

Know that, as I walked upon the Sea of Galilee that I looked up and saw only the power of God. In my heart was naught but a song of praise and love and gratitude, held in complete trust. I did not see the water, nor the storm. Peter looked into the actual conditions of his physical surroundings and began to sink beneath those conditions. Peter saw only the physical. I saw only the Spiritual. The condition for both of us was exactly the same. Peter had the same powers I had but was not aware of it. They were his to use, even as they were mine to use, and as they are yours.

Beloved, if your troubles and storms have turned into a tempest that threatens your destruction, know that I ride upon the storm, and so can you ride upon the storm, above it, and beyond it, if you will only lift your consciousness above the waves and the turmoil, to Me.

Open up your souls that I may tell you how it is done.

There are two kinds of gratitude. One is of the mind and deals with the ordinary gifts of the flesh. This gratitude is the appreciation of the tangible gifts. It is for food, shelter, clothing, friends and all physical and financial blessings and deals with the ordinary comforts and necessities of everyday living. It is of the earth.

The other gratitude is of the soul and swings far out beyond the tangible earthly conditions and circumstances. This gratitude is the great song of ecstasy singing in the soul. It is not hampered nor measured by details. It includes all things. When one has this he is truly thankful in all things. This is the gratitude Paul admonished you to develop when he asked you to thank God in the Spirit when you received blessings.

This gratitude is "The thankfulness that will make you glorious and multiply the blessings of earth an hundred-fold yea, more." This is the great Spiritual gratitude Christine Mercie was using when she was lifted from her little bug infested room of depravement and depression into contact with My Spirit. Her's was a gratitude that completely overcame the condition, and it was changed.

This is the gratitude that is so filled with love it can "Come up over" any condition in existence. All adverse conditions and circumstances crumble before it. It is the gratitude that can glorify God in a crust of bread, in pain, in prison. This is the great Spiritual outpouring, from within man that crumbled prison walls in times past. It has opened prison doors and released iron shackles. In this glorifying gratitude the crust is changed to a banquet table with God; the pain is transmuted to an anointing of divine benediction that holds the power of complete healing.

This is the power of Almighty God, our Father, in action in your lives. This is your power of overcoming, or coming up over all things. This is your holy anointing as you learn to hold to it. This power is always yours to use.

This divine, spiritual gratitude is a vibration which contacts the very throne of God and releases all the powers of the Almighty. This vibration is the contact with the oil of my Spirit, and the Holy flame of the Spirit of Almighty God. This vibration of glory is the power by which all things are overcome. This divine, glorious vibration of praise and rejoicing and thanks is My Name, My Great Unspeakable Name, which you are invited to take upon you. It is your own Anointing of Light. Always hold it in your consciousness, or be ever aware of it, and My Spirit will always be with you and your lamps will be filled. Thus your calling and election will be made sure and you shall place all things under your feet as you overcome all things. Lift your consciousness above the storm and the tempest and the sea of impossible conditions and by your gratitude of soul and singing, inner praise you shall walk above the sea, above the distress, above the overwhelming waves and the wind. This is how you walk with me. I am above the storm, above the distress, above every pain, above your poverty and heartbreaks and tears.

You need no longer linger in these conditions of ill and anguish. Lift up your eyes to me. Lift them above the story. Lift them to the very throne of God, and you shall ride upon the storm, for it is given to you to be able to "come over" it through your loving gratitude and singing song of ecstasy. This great vibration is My Holy Name and it is my Holy Oil of Anointing upon you. Amen.

And so that you may be left without excuse I now give you the three tests by which you may know the truth of my Words.

First: ask of me, with a sincere heart, whether this is of God or not, and He will reveal the truth of it unto you by the power of the Holy Ghost. And thus you may know the truth of all things. But be careful that after such witness is borne to you and testifies to your soul, and brings peace to your heart, by the power of the Holy Ghost, lest you return to your doubting, and thus be found to sin against this Divine Witness, even the Holy Ghost, which sin cannot be forgiven.

Second: Live the teachings and you will KNOW whether they be of God, or whether they be of man.

Third: This is the test that cannot fail, nor can a fool err therein, nor be deceived, for it is as plain to discern as it is to discern the light of noonday from the darkness of night. "Anything that enticeth a man to serve and love God, and to pray, IS OF GOD."

So be it, for I have spoken. Let none mock my words for they are true and faithful.

Yea, I am Jesus Christ, the Beginning and the End, the Alpha and Omega, the great Amen.